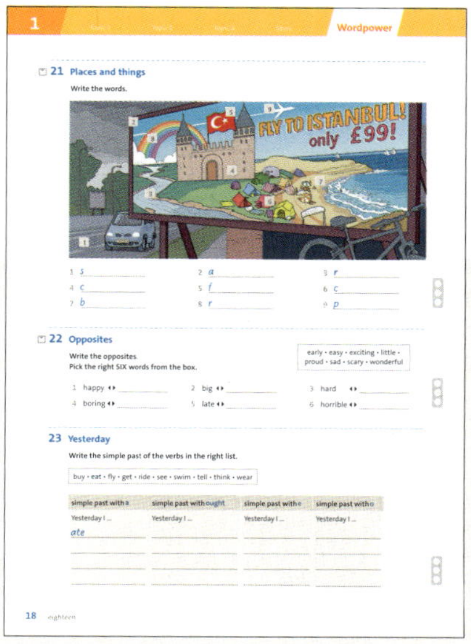

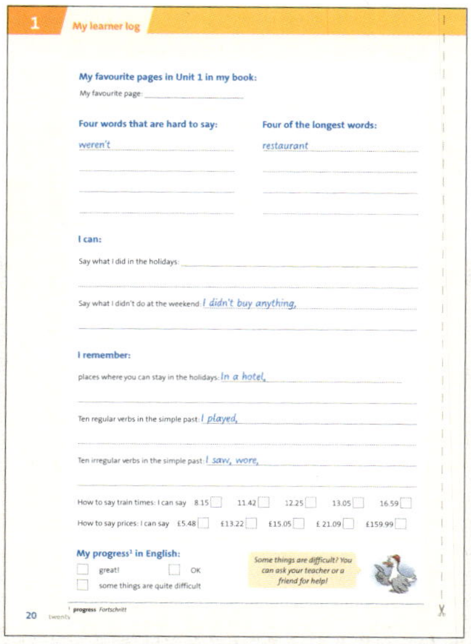

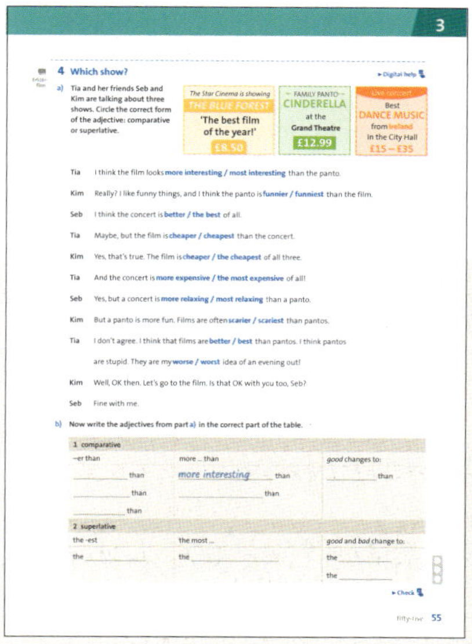

Wordpower

Auf diesen Seiten findest du Übungen zu den Vokabeln der jeweiligen Units und kannst dein gesprochenes Englisch verbessern.

My learner log

Hier kannst du auf die Unit zurückblicken und deinen Lernstand festhalten.

Revision

Halte auf diesen Seiten inne und wiederhole, was du in den vorherigen Units gelernt hast.

Dein Buch findest du auch in der *Cornelsen Lernen App*

Siehst du eines dieser Symbole in deinem Workbook, kannst du in deiner App …

Erklär-film

alle Hörtexte und Videos zu deinem Buch aufrufen.

▶ **Digital help**

auf Ideen und Hilfen zugreifen.

▶ **Check**

deine Antworten eigenständig überprüfen.

lighthouse 2

Workbook

Im Auftrag des Verlages erarbeitet von
Gwen Berwick, York
Sydney Thorne, York

In Zusammenarbeit mit der Englischredaktion
Klaus Unger (Projektleitung),
Karin Wedepohl (verantwortliche Redakteurin), Lisa Ahmadi,
Chiara Castellano, Michael Dunkel

Beratende Mitwirkung
Sabine Bay, Cloppenburg; Ulrike Plänker, Sprockhövel

Medienmanagement
Silke Kirchhoff

Illustrationen
Harald Ardeias, Schelklingen; Josephine Bienert-Köhler, Berlin;
Irina Zinner, Hamburg

Fotos
Anja Poehlmann, Brighton

Für die freundliche Unterstützung danken wir der
Varndean School, Brighton

Umschlaggestaltung
Rosendahl, Berlin

Layoutkonzept
Klein & Halm, Berlin

Layout und technische Umsetzung
Straive

Passend zum Workbook:
Sprechen, Aussprache, Wortschatz und Grammatik digital üben mit der mobilen App ChatClass. Erhältlich auch als PrintPlus-Lizenz bei Nutzung des Arbeitsheftes.

www.cornelsen.de

Druck: ppm Fulda GmbH & Co. KG, Fulda

1. Auflage, 1. Druck 2023
Workbook 2
ISBN 978-3-06-035776-5

1. Auflage, 1. Druck 2023
Workbook 2 Lehrkräftefassung
ISBN 978-3-06-035778-9

PEFC-zertifiziert
Dieses Produkt stammt aus nachhaltig bewirtschafteten Wäldern, Recycling und kontrollierten Quellen
PEFC
PEFC/04-31-1308
www.pefc.de

BASIC lighthouse 2

Workbook

Audios online verfügbar unter
www.cornelsen.de/webcodes **Code:** bowazu

Dein Workbook findest du auch in der Cornelsen Lernen App.

Siehst du eines dieser Symbole in deinem Workbook, findest du in der App …

- alle **Audios**
- alle **Videos** und **Erklärfilme**
- **Hilfen** und **Lösungen** zu ausgewählten Aufgaben

Cornelsen

Titelbild

Cornelsen/Personen am Strand: Anja Poehlmann, Strandhäuschen: Shutterstock.com/JoolsW

Illustrationen

Cornelsen/Harald Ardeias: (S. 1 (li.); S. 7; S. 9; S. 10 o.r.; S. 15, S. 18; S. 21, S. 23 u.r.; S. 24; S. 27; S. 31 A-H; S. 34 u.r.; S. 38; S. 39 4.1-4.4; S. 42; S. 46; S. 47 A-H; S. 48; S. 50; S. 53; S. 54 u.r.; S. 60; S. 61 m.r.; S. 62; S. 63; S. 65; S. 75 o.r.; S. 74; S. 85); **Cornelsen/Irina Zinner**: S. III; S. 1 (Möwe); S. 5 o.l.; S. 10 o.l.; S. 11 m.r.; S. 13; S. 20; S. 25; S. 61 o.r.; S. 83; S. 84; S. 68; S. 69).

Abbildungen

Umschlaginnenseite vorne (U2): Siehe S. 8, S. 9, S. 81; **S. 5–6:** Cornelsen/Anja Poehlmann; **S. 8:** Shutterstock.com/Peredniankina; **S. 10** u.r.: stock.adobe.com/@CPPHOTOGRAPHIC/Chris; **S. 11** o.r.: mauritius images/Pitopia, u.r.: stock.adobe.com/Andrey Lapshin; **S. 12:** stock.adobe.com/zefart; **S. 14:** Cornelsen/Anja Poehlmann; **S. 16:** Shutterstock.com/Amorn Suriyan; **S. 23** 1, 4: stock.adobe.com/iiierlok_xolms, 2: stock.adobe.com/TALVA, 3: stock.adobe.com/designer_an; **S. 26** 4.1: stock.adobe.com/Peredniankina, 4.2: Shutterstock.com/Max Topchii, 4.3: Shutterstock.com/Erika Cross, 4.4: Shutterstock.com/ANURAK PONGPATIMET; **S. 30:** akg-images/DN/TT News Agency; **S. 31** o.r.: Cornelsen/Inhouse; **S. 32:** Cornelsen/Inhouse; **S. 34** 19.1: stock.adobe.com/Marina Lohrbach, 19.2: stock.adobe.com/cynoclub, 19.3: stock.adobe.com/Kathrin39, 19.4: Shutterstock.com/Kapitula Olga, 19.5: Shutterstock.com/photobeps, 19.6: stock.adobe.com/baibaz, 19.7: Shutterstock.com/Stocksnapper, 19.8: Shutterstock.com/Ko Backpacko, 19.9: Shutterstock.com/ozanuysal, 20.1: Shutterstock.com/Roman Samborskyi, 20.2: Shutterstock.com/Roman Samborskyi, 20.3: Shutterstock.com/Roman Samborskyi, 20.4: Shutterstock.com/Casther, 20.5: Shutterstock.com/goldenfish_27, 20.6: Shutterstock.com/ErsinTekkol, 20.7: Shutterstock.com/Gladius Stock, 20.8: Shutterstock.com/vectorlab2D, 20.9: Shutterstock.com/Cookie Studio; **S. 35** o.r.: Shutterstock.com/Just dance, u.r.: stock.adobe.com/tgordievskaya; **S. 37:** akg-images/TT NEWS AGENCY; **S. 39** 5.1-5.6: Shutterstock.com/Noch; **S. 40:** Imago Stock & People GmbH/ZUMA Press; **S. 41** A: stock.adobe.com/Pavel Losevsky, B: Shutterstock.com/Rittis, C: Shutterstock.com/fotoknips, D: stock.adobe.com/matimix, E: stock.adobe.com/Mary, F: Shutterstock.com/Pazargic Liviu; **S. 43** m.r.: stock.adobe.com//Irin Fierce, 8: Shutterstock.com/Azizah's; **S. 44** u.l.: Shutterstock.com/VanderWolf Images, 1: mauritius images/Science Source, 2: stock.adobe.com/nahhan, 3: stock.adobe.com/Peter Hermes Furian, 4: Shutterstock.com/Catarina Belova; **S. 45:** Shutterstock.com/Monkey Business Images; **S. 47** 4: stock.adobe.com/Brocreative, 5: Shutterstock.com/PhotoRoman, 6: stock.adobe.com/Mary, 7: Shutterstock.com/EFKS; **S. 52** 1–2: stock.adobe.com/WONG SZE FEI, 3: Shutterstock.com/szefei; **S. 54** 1–4: Shutterstock.com/Azizah's; **S. 56** A: stock.adobe.com/Gino Santa Maria, B: stock.adobe.com/Paul Lawrenson 2017/Paul, C: stock.adobe.com/weyo, D: stock.adobe.com/jessicagirvan, E: stock.adobe.com/aamulya, F: stock.adobe.com/Ruth Black; **S. 57** 3.1: Shutterstock.com/Perutskyi Petro, 3.2: Shutterstock.com/Peter Hermes Furian, 4.6: stock.adobe.com/Nataliia Pyzhova, 3.3: Shutterstock.com/MaraZe, 3.4: Shutterstock.com/Nataly Studio, 3.5: Shutterstock.com/paulista, 3.6: Shutterstock.com/Svetlana Serebryakova, 4.1: Shutterstock.com/Anna Kucherova, 4.2: stock.adobe.com/volff, 4.3: stock.adobe.com/praha.cz/etienne@vosk/Moving Moment, 4.4: Shutterstock.com/azure1, 4.5: Shutterstock.com/Anton Starikov; **S. 58** 1: stock.adobe.com/Irina, 2: Shutterstock.com/CKP1001, 3: Shutterstock.com/vm2002; **S. 64** A: Shutterstock.com/Eric Isselee, B: Shutterstock.com/Aksenova Natalya, C: Shutterstock.com/New Africa, D: Shutterstock.com/Anton 246; **S. 66** 1: stock.adobe.com/moonkin, 2: stock.adobe.com/VectorBum, 3: Shutterstock.com, 4: stock.adobe.com/Stalvalki, 5: stock.adobe.com/inspiring.team, 6: stock.adobe.com/MicroOne, apple: Shutterstock.com/grey_and, jogurt: Shutterstock.com/mexrix, eggs: Shutterstock.com/GSDesign, strawberries: Shutterstock.com/Maks Narodenko, melon: Shutterstock.com/MaraZe, butter: Shutterstock.com/Tanya Sid, flour: Shutterstock.com/Seregam, cheese: Shutterstock.com/Volodymyr Krasyuk, cream: Shutterstock.com/Nattika; **S. 67** 1: Shutterstock.com/xiaorui, 2: Shutterstock.com/Adisa, 3: Shutterstock.com/Romariolen, 4: Shutterstock.com/DenisProduction.com; **S. 70** u.l.: Shutterstock.com/mavo, 1 a: Shutterstock.com/Teguh Mujiono, 2 a: Shutterstock.com/Teguh Mujiono, 3 a: Shutterstock.com/Teguh Mujiono, 4 a: stock.adobe.com/inspiring.team, 5 a: stock.adobe.com/inspiring.team, 1 b: Shutterstock.com/EM Arts, 2 b: Shutterstock.com/Evgeny Karandaev, 3 b: Shutterstock.com/SOMMAI, 4 b: Shutterstock.com/Seregam, 5 b: Shutterstock.com/Nattika, 6 b: Shutterstock.com/HomeStudio; **S. 71** 1: Shutterstock.com/PeopleImages.com - Yuri A, 2: Shutterstock.com/Pixel-Shot, 3: Shutterstock.com/New Africa, 4: Shutterstock.com/Ekaterina Beaver, 5: Shutterstock.com/Alexander Raths, 6: Shutterstock.com/Stokkete, 7: Shutterstock.com/Yuliia D, 8: Shutterstock.com/Sergii Kumer; **S. 75** m.r.: Shutterstock.com/Chrispictures; **S. 76** A: Shutterstock.com/Monkey Business Images, B: Shutterstock.com/fizkes, C: Shutterstock.com/Olena Ivanova, D: Shutterstock.com/Africa Studio, E+F: Shutterstock.com/Pixel-Shot, G: Shutterstock.com/Alina Kruk, H: Shutterstock.com/Tatyana Dzemileva, I: Shutterstock.com/Sandra van der Steen, J: Shutterstock.com/Denis Mamin; **S. 77** 11.1: Shutterstock.com/LemonadePixel, 11.2: stock.adobe.com/Tartila, 11.3: Shutterstock.com/LemonadePixel; **S. 78:** Shutterstock.com/rangizzz; **S. 81:** Cornelsen/Grasshopper Films LTD; **S. 82:** Shutterstock.com/okili77; **S. 86:** stock.adobe.com/zefart; **S. 87** o.r.: Cornelsen/Inhouse; 1: Shutterstock.com/Perutskyi Petro, 2: Shutterstock.com/Ailisa, 3: stock.adobe.com/Baiba Opule/baibaz, 4: Shutterstock.com/Svetlana Serebryakova, 5: stock.adobe.com/karandaev, 6: stock.adobe.com/Pictures/EKH/EKH-Pictures; **S. 88** 1: Shutterstock.com/LemonadePixel, 2: Shutterstock.com/VikiVector, 3: Shutterstock.com/LemonadePixel

Hello again!
The last day of the holidays

1 Ready for school

► SB, p. 10

01

a) LISTENING Read sentences 1–6 below. Listen again to Zane, Noah and Sunita and circle the right answer.

1 Zane is with Lily in the park / at the beach.

2 Zane and Lily want to go back to school / don't want to go back to school.

3 Noah has a new school bag / his old school bag.

4 Sunita is in town with Willow / her mum.

5 She's looking for a new pencil case / school tie.

6 She can't wait to see her cousins / her friends at school.

b) Now write the words in the right columns.

places	people	school things

bag • beach • friends • home • mum • pencil case • school • town • uniform

2 LANGUAGE The four friends

► SB, p. 10

Write about the four friends.
Use the words from the box.

~~are~~ • has • her • his • is • she • they

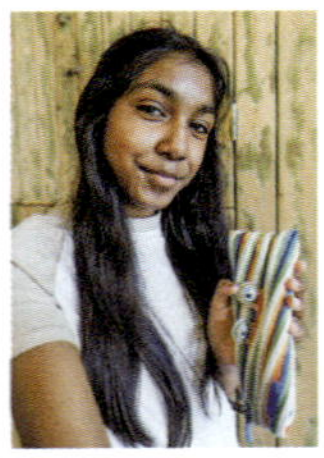

Lily and Zane (1) *are* ______ at the beach.

(2) ______ are enjoying the last day of the holidays.

Noah (3) ______ at home. He's wearing (4) ______ new school uniform.

He (5) ______ a new school bag too.

Sunita is in town. (6) ______ can't wait to see all (7) ______ friends at school.

3 A day at Brighton beach

► SB, p.11

a) **Read the sentences below. Six words are different from the listening text. Circle the six words if you can remember them.**

1 You're sitting on the beach in Brighton. You can see the clear green water of the sea.

2 Listen: Can you hear the sound of the wind? Can you taste the salt from the water? Can you see fish?

3 Listen to the people in the water. They're swimming and playing and they're very happy. Can you hear them?

4 Now you're standing in the sea. The water feels cool on your hands. Can you feel the water?

02 b) LISTENING **Listen again and read the sentences above. Circle the six words that are different from the listening text or check if you circled the six right words.**

c) **Now read the text below. Can you fill the gaps with the right beach words?**

Look up! (1) Seagulls are flying over the (2) ______ and the (3) ______.

Look at them, look how high they are flying, look how free they are. Can you see them?

There's a little bit of (4) ______. Can you feel the (5) ______? It feels nice and warm.

Now you're looking at the (6) ______. It's the afternoon, but there are a lot of lights

and a lot of different colours. There is loud dance music – can you hear it?

Families are walking on the pier. They're wearing (7) ______ hats and they're eating hot dogs.

Your sister is waving to you, she has an ice cream for you. It tastes wonderful.

It tastes of summer (8) ______.

03 d) **Listen again and check your answers.**

I can **talk about summer activities.**

Unit 1
Travel and holidays

1 On holiday

► SB, p. 13

Look at the words in the box. Then write them in the right list.

amazing • at home • Austria • boring • brother • campsite • cold • ~~cool~~ • fun • holiday apartment • horrible • hot • ~~hotel~~ • ~~mum~~ • parents • Poland • rainy • sister • ~~Spain~~ • ~~sunny~~ • Turkey • Wales • windy

country	weather	place to stay	family	how was it?
Spain	*sunny*	*hotel*	*mum*	*cool*

2 READING Oscar's holidays

► SB, p. 13

Read about Oscar's holidays. Then answer the questions. Short answers are OK.

At the end of July I was at my grandma's house in Watford. It was a great week, with one amazing day in London. I was lucky, because it was sunny every day.
In August I was in Spain for two weeks with my parents, my brother Freddie and my sister Olivia. We were in a little hotel. We weren't next to the sea, but near the sea. It was really hot and sunny, but often cloudy in the evenings.

1 When was Oscar in Watford? ______

2 Why was Oscar lucky? ______

3 Where was Oscar for two weeks in August? ______

4 Where was their hotel? ______

5 What was the weather like? ______

I can talk about my holidays and the weather.

Erklär-
film

3 LANGUAGE Simple past: positive Oscar and his family in Spain

► SB p. 15

What did Oscar and his family do on their holiday in Spain? Write a sentence for each picture. Use the words in the box.

We	listened stayed sunbathed watched enjoyed liked	our holiday very much. dancers in the street. the amazing ice cream. on a campsite in Spain. on the beach. to flamenco music.

1  *We stayed on a campsite in Spain.*

2  ______________________

3  ______________________

4  ______________________

5  ______________________

6  ______________________

4 LANGUAGE Simple past: positive My holiday at home last year

► SB, p. 15

Write the nine regular verbs in the simple past.

I (1) *stayed* (stay) at home in the holidays last year and it wasn't boring! I (2) ______ (cycle) every day,

I (3) ______ (listen) to some of my favourite podcasts and

I (4) ______ (start) to play the guitar.

I also (5) ______ (help) mum a bit at home.

I (6) ______ (cook) some meals and

I sometimes (7) ______ (remember) to put out the rubbish!

And I (8) ______ (play) a lot with our cat.

I (9) ______ (love) doing that! – Holidays? I was really busy!!

> **!**
> Regular verbs in the simple past:
> (verb) + ed
> (verb ends in e) + d

5 Listening A scary holiday story

🔊 04

► SB, p. 16

a) **Oscar's friend Ling tells you about her holiday in Whitby, a town in the north of England. Listen to her and tick (✓) the right sentence A–D.**

Always read the sentences before you listen!

1 Ling was in Whitby, in the north of England, ...
- A last summer. ☐
- B last winter. ☐
- C in April this year. ☐

2 Ling and her family were ...
- A in a hotel. ☐
- B in a holiday apartment. ☐
- C on a campsite. ☐

3 In Whitby ...
- A Ling's family were the only tourists. ☐
- B there were many other visitors. ☐
- C there were no tourists in the shops. ☐

4 Ling knows the story of Dracula because ...
- A she watched the film. ☐
- B her teacher told the story in class. ☐
- C she has the book. ☐

5 In the film, Dracula ...
- A was a big black cat. ☐
- B played with dogs. ☐
- C did horrible things. ☐

6 Now Ling ...
- A is too scared to watch the film again. ☐
- B wants to get the book. ☐
- C wants to buy a Dracula game. ☐

b) **Listen again and circle the right answer.**

1 Whitby is ...

nice when it's sunny / always really dark.

2 Dracula the vampire ...

was nice at first / travelled to England.

3 In Whitby, Dracula was ...

an animal / a person.

4 The guide ...

looked like Dracula / had stories about Dracula.

6 LANGUAGE Simple past: positive A holiday in Italy

► SB, p. 17

did • had • said • saw • told • went

a) Write the simple past forms of the verbs. Choose the right forms from the box.

	simple past:		simple past:
do	______	say	______
go	______	tell	______
have	______	see	______

Italy

b) Now complete the sentences with the correct verbs from a).

1 In my holiday last year I ______ (go) to Italy with my family.

2 We ______ (see) some really nice places.

3 And we ______ (do) fun activities in the sea.

4 Somebody at the hotel ______ (tell) us where to buy the best food!

5 We all ______ (have) a really good time.

6 We all ______ (say) Italy was great and we want to go again next year!

7 LANGUAGE Simple past: positive Oscar's holiday in October

► SB, p. 17

a) Read the text and look at the verbs in blue.

Circle the regular verbs (simple past with *-ed*) and underline the irregular verbs (special forms).

Regular verbs have simple past forms with -ed. But irregular verbs have special forms!

In my week's holiday I (1) *stayed* (stay) at home.

Some days I (2) ______ (play) with my brother and sister

and we (3) ______ (watch) some films together.

We (4) ______ (have) good fun.

My mum and dad (5) ______ (work) on most days,

but we (6) ______ (do) something together on Friday:

we all (7) ______ (go) to a show in London.

The music (8) ______ (be) great. I really (9) ______ (enjoy) it.

b) Now write the correct forms of the verbs in the simple past.

I can write about my holiday activities.

8 LISTENING Times

05–08

► Digital help ► SB, p. 18

- Choose five times: 9.15 9.50 10.08 10.18 11.14 11.40 12.20 1.12 1.32 2.10 2.59. Write them in the boxes.
- Play the game in groups. Listen. When you hear your times, cross them out (~~9.15~~).
- If you hear all five times, shout "Here!". The game ends – you win!

Game 1

Game 2

Game 3

Game 4

9 LISTENING AND SPEAKING Train times

► SB, p. 18

a) **Partner B: Look at page 86.**

Partner A: Listen to Partner B. Write the times of the trains.

Train to Brighton: ______________

Train to Hastings: ______________

Train to Eastbourne: ______________

Train to Portsmouth: ______________

b) **The train to Brighton is late. Ask your partner about it and write the information.**

Excuse me, please. When is the next train to Brighton?

new arrival time is ______________

new platform: ______________

c) **Look at the information and read the train station announcements[1].**

The next train to Woking is at 19.05 at platform 3. Platform 3 for the 19.05 train to Woking.

The next train to Gatwick Airport is at ... at platform ... Platform ... for the ... train to ...

The next train to ... is ...

Woking 19.05	Platform 3
Gatwick Airport 18.48	Platform 1
Epsom 18.59	Platform 11
Dorking 19.12	Platform 8
(For Dorking change in Redhill.)	

d) **Look at the information in c) and answer your partner's question.**

e) **Now check your answers with your partner.**

[1] **announcement** *Durchsage*

10 At the station

► SB, p. 19

a) **Complete the dialogue with words from the box.**

at • good • please • return • train • when

For 15.02 you say fifteen – O – two.
For £10.09 you say ten pounds and nine p.

Tourist Excuse me, please. ________ is the next train to York?

Official It's ___ 15.02. Do you want a single or ________ ticket?

Tourist A single ticket, ________.

Official That's £10.09, please.

Tourist Here you are. What platform is the ______ to York?

Official Platform 4. Have a ______ journey!

b) SPEAKING **Now practise the dialogue with a partner. Change the words in blue.**

1	2	3	4
to Bristol at 9.17	to Manchester at 2.32	to Leeds at 3.07	to Liverpool at 21.24
single ticket	return ticket	return ticket	single ticket
platform 7	platform 3	platform 7	platform 1
£31.75	£19.12	£17.48	£8.06

11 MEDIATION All about *Pride*

► SB, p. 20

You were at the *Pride* parade with Lily and her friends.
Answer these questions from a friend in Germany.
Tip: Use the information on pages 18 and 20 in your book.

Freund *Pride* Parade klingt interessant. Wie groß ist sie in Brighton?

Du ______________________________

Viele Menschen hatten Fahnen. Aber meine Freundin Lily hat keine Fahne gekauft.

Freund Nein? Warum nicht?

Du ______________________________

Und irrsinnig laut war es! Dabei kann mein Freund Noah Lärm gar nicht ertragen!

Freund Echt? Wie hat er es denn ausgehalten?

Du ______________________________

Freund Was konnte man machen, nachdem der Umzug vorbei war?

Du ______________________________

12 LANGUAGE Simple past: negative Brighton *Pride*

Erklär-film

► SB, p. 20

a) **Look again at the text on page 20 in your book. What's true? Circle the right answer.**

Lily (1) went / didn't go with her mum and dad.

She (2) went / didn't go with her friends.

Sunita (3) bought / didn't buy a *Pride* flag.

Lily (4) bought / didn't buy anything.

Noah (5) wore / didn't wear headphones.

Lily and her friends (6) watched / didn't watch the people in the parade, but they (7) saw / didn't see their friend Willow and her girlfriend. They (8) ate / didn't eat rainbow cake in the Family *Pride* area. After the parade they (9) listened / didn't listen to street musicians, but (10) went / didn't go to the concert.

b) **Now check your answers on page 20 in your book.**

13 LANGUAGE Simple past (negative) Ling and Oscar's weekends

► SB, p. 20

a) **Read the sentences about Ling. Write the verbs 3–8.**

b) **Oscar didn't do what Ling did. Complete the sentences about Oscar in the simple past.**

Ling	Verb	Oscar
1 Ling did her homework.	do	1 Oscar didn't do his homework.
2 She texted her friends.	text	2 He ________ his friends.
3 She ate some cake.	________	3 He ________ cake.
4 She listened to music.	________	4 He ________ to music.
5 She went into town.	________	5 He ________ into town.
6 She saw a friend in town.	________	6 He ________ a friend in town.
7 She bought a present.	________	7 He ________ a present.
8 She had a great time.	________	8 He ________ a great time.

14 Words in Unit 1

▶ SB, p. 20

Write the words in the crossword.

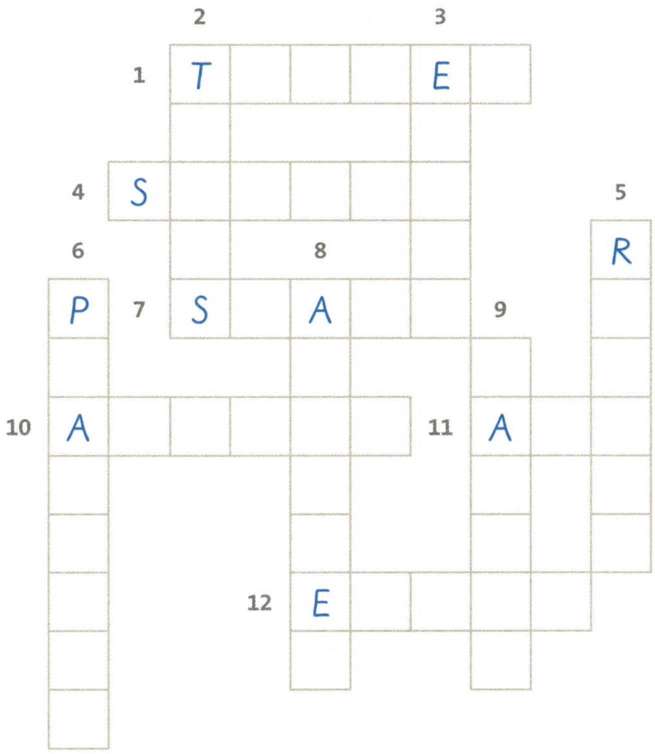

1 When you travel by train you must have a ...

2 journeys

3 24/7 = ... day of the week

4 a one way ticket

5 The Rhine, the Amazon and the Nile are three ...

6 the place in the station where you wait for the train

7 Are you scared of vampires? Many people people think vampires are ...

8 The 'arrivals' tell you when your train ...

9 

10 the longer word for an 'ad'

11 past tense of eat

12 the opposite of late

15 LANGUAGE Simple past (negative) Your weekend

▶ Digital help ▶ SB, p. 20

a) **Write two things which you did and two things which you didn't do last weekend!**

- I went shopping with ... / I ...
- I watched / ...
- I didn't visit / listen to ... / ...

____

____

____

____

____

b) WALK AROUND **Say your sentences to other students. Can you find another student with one of your sentences?**

I went into town.

Me too! I went into town too!

And I watched a film.

Ah, sorry! I didn't watch a film!

I can **talk about a special day in my holidays.**

16 Reading **Oscar's idea**

► SB, p. 23

Read Oscar's article and sentences 1–6 below. Are the sentences true (T) or false (F)? Highlight the places in the article which give you the information.

1 The woman from 'Keep Britain Tidy' talked to Oscar and his friends in his home.
2 At first Oscar didn't think that the woman was right.
3 Oscar and his friends had rubbish-pickers from their parents.
4 There were a lot of plastic bags in the rubbish.
5 After their work Oscar and his friends ate some things.
6 Oscar says that people think too much about rubbish.

Die Antworten stehen nicht immer genau wörtlich im Text, z. B.: not right (in der Frage) = wrong (im Text).

www.schoolpaper.example.com

My big idea – *by Oscar*

About six months ago a woman from a group called "Keep[1] Britain Tidy" came to my school and talked to us about the problem of rubbish. She told us that people drop[2] two million pieces of rubbish in Britain every day: in towns, next to roads, on the beaches etc. 'Do something about rubbish!' was her message.

Two million pieces? "She's wrong," I said to Ling. So after school I looked online and I saw that she was right! 'That's terrible,' I thought. 'What can I do?'

Next to our school there is a place where people stop and have picnics. And there is always a lot of rubbish there – pieces of paper, cans, plastic bottles and things like that. So some friends and I made a plan and we told other students about it. We borrowed[3] rubbish-pickers[4] from a place in town, we bought some big black plastic bags and one Saturday morning we all arrived in the field, put on our gloves and began to pick rubbish.

I was surprised to find so much rubbish and so many plastic bags. I thought people didn't use plastic bags any more. And I was angry. I thought, 'With so much rubbish everywhere, animals and children can't use places like this. That's terrible!' We had different bags for plastic bottles, for aluminium cans and for the rest of the rubbish. And when we stopped we had ten bags in all. Then we had a picnic, with sandwiches, crisps, fruit, chocolate, etc. – and of course we put all the paper and plastic in our bags!

Three months later our little group got a prize. I was proud of what we did, but I am still angry. Why is there so much rubbish everywhere? Don't people see it? Or don't they think when they drop a can or a plastic bottle? How can people be so stupid?

Source: https://www.keepbritaintidy.org/faqs/advice/litter-and-law#:~:text=More%20than%20two%20million%20pieces,look%20untidy%20and%20uncared%20for (31.01.2023)

[1] **keep** *behalten* [2] **drop** *fallen lassen* [3] **borrow** **ausleihen** [4] **rubbish-picker** *Müllsammler*

I can **talk about last weekend.**

17 READING What is the story about?

► SB, pp. 24–26

Look at the story on pages 24–25 in your book. Texts A, B, C are all true. Tick (✓) the text that tells the story best.

A
It's about Noah's first train journey alone and about all the nice things he did when he was with Buddy and his grandma in Portsmouth. ☐

B
It's about how Noah, after a nice day in Portsmouth, was alone in a scary situation. But he did the right thing, his friends helped him and he felt good in the end. ☐

C
The story is about how travelling by train can be difficult because it is so easy to get on the wrong train. And then you are in real trouble. ☐

18 READING Tell the story

► SB, pp. 24–26

Answer the questions. Short answers are OK.

1 Why does Noah not see his grandma very often? ______

2 Who travelled with Noah by train? ______

3 What did Noah do in Portsmouth? ______

4 What did Noah do in the wrong train? ______

5 How did Noah's friends help him? ______

6 How did Noah's parents feel when Noah arrived in Brighton? ______

19 Language in the story

► Digital help ► SB, pp. 24–26

Write the simple past forms of the verbs. They are all in the story.

1 travel *(part 1)* – ______
2 get on *(part 2)* – ______
3 swim *(part 2)* – ______
4 take *(part 3)* – ______
5 put *(part 5)* – ______
6 arrive *(part 6)* – ______

20 What do you think?

► Digital help SB, pp. 24–26

Complete the sentences. You can use words from the box for the first part of the sentences.

brave • friendly • helpful • kind • mean • ...

1 I think Noah was ______ because ______.

2 I think Noah's friends were ______ because ______.

I can talk about new experiences.

21 Places and things

Write the words.

1 *s* ______ 2 *a* ______ 3 *r* ______
4 *c* ______ 5 *f* ______ 6 *c* ______
7 *b* ______ 8 *r* ______ 9 *p* ______

22 Opposites

Write the opposites.
Pick the right SIX words from the box.

early • easy • exciting • little • proud • sad • scary • wonderful

1 happy ◂▸ ______ 2 big ◂▸ ______ 3 hard ◂▸ ______
4 boring ◂▸ ______ 5 late ◂▸ ______ 6 horrible ◂▸ ______

23 Yesterday

Write the simple past of the verbs in the right list.

buy • ~~eat~~ • fly • get • ride • see • swim • tell • think • wear

simple past with a	simple past with ought	simple past with e	simple past with o
Yesterday I ...	Yesterday I ...	Yesterday I ...	Yesterday I ...
ate			

24 Funny plural forms (not just -s)

Write the plural forms of these words. Use every "e" in the box. Cross out an "e" each time you use one.

e • e • e • e • e • e • e • e • e

1 foot – ______ 2 shelf – ______ 3 penny – ______

4 tooth – ______ 5 fish – ______ 6 mouse – ______

25 Word groups

Write the words in the network.

angry • arrival • at 2 o'clock • at night • boat • calm • car • in the evening • ferry • plane • platform • return • scared • single • worried • yesterday

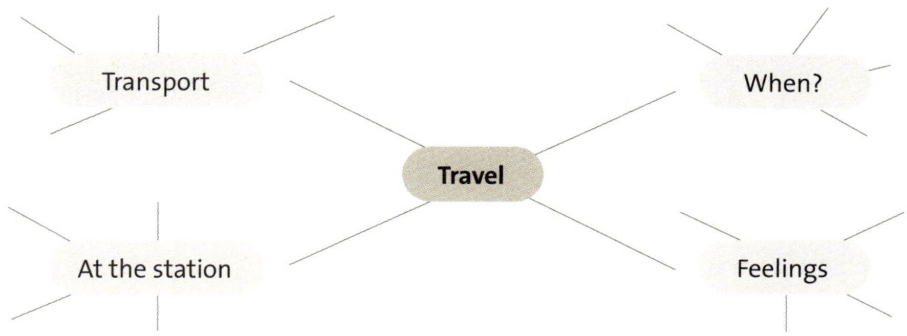

26 Speaking Speak English well: The letter "O"

09 a) **Listen to the five words. How many different ways of saying the letter „O" do you hear?**

love hot do go brother 1 ☐ 2 ☐ 3 ☐ 4 ☐ 5 ☐

b) **Write the words in the right groups.** ▸ Digital help

another	bottle	glove	hope	hospital
money	move	only	podcast	shoe
told	two	who	wonderful	wrong

O as in love [ʌ]: ______

O as in hot [ɒ]: ______

O as in do [uː]: ______

O as in go [əʊ]: ______

10 c) **Listen and check your answers.**

11 d) **Listen again and repeat the words.**

e) **Write a (funny) sentence with as many words from b) as you can!**

______

______

My favourite pages in Unit 1 in my book:

My favourite page: ____________________

Four words that are hard to say:

weren't

____

____

____

Four of the longest words:

restaurant

____

____

____

I can:

Say what I did in the holidays: ____________________

____

Say what I didn't do at the weekend: *I didn't buy anything,*

____

I remember:

places where you can stay in the holidays: *In a hotel,*

____

Ten regular verbs in the simple past: *I played,*

____

Ten irregular verbs in the simple past: *I saw, wore,*

____

How to say train times: I can say 8.15 ☐ 11.42 ☐ 12.25 ☐ 13.05 ☐ 16.59 ☐

How to say prices: I can say £5.48 ☐ £13.22 ☐ £15.05 ☐ £ 21.09 ☐ £159.99 ☐

My progress[1] in English:

☐ great! ☐ OK

☐ some things are quite difficult

Some things are difficult? You can ask your teacher or a friend for help!

[1] **progress** *Fortschritt*

1 Can you complete the ghost tour?

▸ Digital help

Start your ghost tour at START. There are ten ghosts[1]. Each ghost makes you say four things.

- If you can say all four things, tick (✓) the box and you can move to the next ghost.
- If you can't, you can look in your book and find the answers. Then go on to the next ghost.

Can you complete the ghost tour?

▸ Check

[1] **ghost** *Gespenst*

Erklär-film

1 Verbs in the simple past

a) **Look at the verbs in blue in the text in 1b).**
Verbs with simple past -ed → underline
Verbs with special forms → circle

> **!**
> In the simple past
> – some verbs end in -ed.
> – some verbs have special forms.

b) **Now write the correct forms of the verbs in the simple past.**

Last night I (1) *stayed* ____ (stay) at home and (2) ____________ (listen) to music in my room.

I also (3) ____________ (do) my maths homework and then I (4) ____________ (watch) a film

and (5) ____________ (play) a game.

Then I (6) ____________ (go) to bed.

It (7) ____________ (be) cold in bed, so I (8) ____________ (wear) my warm pyjamas!

2 More verbs in the simple past

Write the verbs in the simple past in the puzzle.

1 fly
2 be *(they, we, you)*
3 find
4 put
5 think
6 buy
7 *(across)* go
7 *(down)* wear
8 *(across)* say
8 *(down)* swim
9 make
10 ride
11 do
12 eat
13 see
14 have
15 get

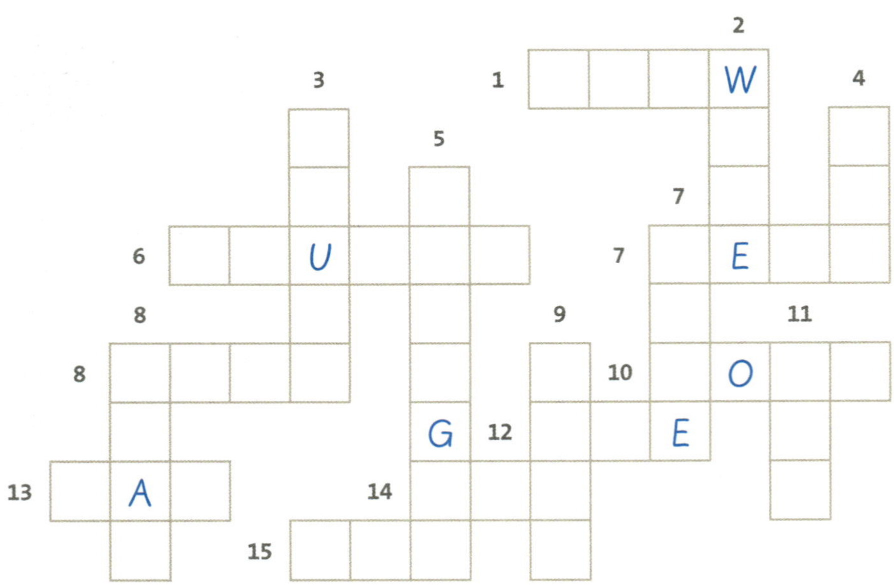

> All the verbs have special forms in the simple past. Not sure about them? Look at page 271 in your book.

▸ Check

Erklär-film

3 Tia's family holiday

▶ Digital help

Tia's holiday went wrong. Write the six verbs in the negative simple past.

1 We went to Italy by train. We *didn't go by plane.*

2 We stayed in a hotel. We ______________________ on a campsite.

3 We swam in the hotel pool. We ______________________ in the sea.

4 We had a lot of rain. We ______________________ a lot of sun.

5 The holiday was OK. It ______________________ wonderful.

6 The people in the hotel were OK. But they ______________________ very friendly.

!
Remember:
I saw
→ I didn't see
I played
→ I didn't play
It was great.
→ It wasn't great.
They were here.
→ They weren't here.

4 At the station

Tia helps a tourist at the station. Complete the dialogue with words from the box.

arrive • ~~help~~ • machine • next • platform • return • welcome

Tia Hi. Can I (1) *help* you?

Tourist Yes, thanks. I need a ticket to Manchester. But I don't know how to use this ticket (2) ______________.

Tia No problem. Do you want a single or a (3) ______________ ?

Tourist Just a single, please.

Tia Look, a single ticket to Manchester costs £27.50.

Tourist Thank you. And when is the (4) ______________ train to Manchester?

Tia Let me see ... In twenty minutes, from (5) ______________ 3.

Tourist And when does it (6) ______________ in Manchester?

Tia Look, it tells you here. At half past four.

Tourist Thank you so much!

Tia You're very (7) ______________. Bye!

▶ Check

Unit 2
Friends and heroes

1 LISTENING The head students in Varndean School

12

► SB, p. 41

Listen to Lily, Noah, Sunita and Zane. (Circle) the correct answer.

1 **Zane** Head students are students in year 10 / year 11.

2 **Noah** That boy, there ... He has short dark / blond hair.

3 **Zane** That's Mihai. He's the head student for our class / house.

4 **Lily** You see that girl? She's wearing a blue / green tie and glasses.

5 **Zane** I don't know who the other girl is. She has long straight / curly hair and glasses.

6 **Sunita** That's Faye. My brother Nish knows / likes her.

2 Describing people

► SB, p. 42

a) **Match the descriptions to the pictures.**

A This student has short hair. She doesn't have glasses, and she doesn't have braces. She's wearing a green sweatshirt. Picture ☐	B This student is wearing a blue T-shirt. He has long curly dark hair and looks friendly. He has brown eyes and he has glasses. Picture ☐
C This student has blond hair and blue eyes. He has braces. He doesn't have glasses. Is he big or small? I don't know! Picture ☐	D This student has long straight hair. I think she's often funny. She doesn't have braces and she doesn't have glasses. Picture ☐

b) **And you? Describe yourself: eyes, hair, etc. Tipp: Use language from texts A–D.**

I have ______________________________

I don't have ______________________________

I can describe what someone looks like.

3 What are people like?

▸ SB, p. 43

a) **Look at the words in the box. Then read sentences 1–9 and complete the puzzle with nine words from the box. Cross out (~~cross out~~) the words that you use from the box.**

amazing • brave • ~~clever~~ • fair • funny • helpful • kind • mean • messy • polite • quiet

1 She's good at many different things.

2 He always says 'Please' and 'Thank you'.

3 She always makes me laugh.

4 He doesn't have favourite people. He's the same to everybody.

5 She's just great!

6 She's always nice to people and helps them if they need her.

7 She always says what is right, even if other people laugh at her.

8 He's not nice.

9 She's not loud.

				1	C	L	E	V	E	R
			2							
		3								
				4						
5										
	6									
7										
	8									
9										

b) **Write the word in blue.**

He's calm and always knows what to do: ______________

c) **Now write the two words you didn't use in a) next to the right definitions 1 or 2.**

1 She isn't tidy – she's ____________.

2 She is always very friendly and ________.

Use the words from the box in a). ☺

d) **Now check your answers in a), b) and c) with a partner.**

4 LISTENING Friends

13

► SB, p. 45

a) Alex interviews Oscar, his sister Olivia, his brother Freddie and Ling about their best friends. Listen to them and circle the two correct answers.

1 Oscar says Ling is
- A polite.
- B funny.
- C kind.

2 Freddie says his mum is
- A happy.
- B honest.
- C fair.

3 Olivia says her friend Jessie is
- A quiet.
- B confident.
- C brave.

4 Ling says Oscar is
- A sometimes angry.
- B sometimes mean.
- C good fun.

b) Listen again and complete the sentences below with one word.

1 Oscar says, "Ling always does nice things for people. I think that's *i* ____________."

2 Freddie says, "Mum is the *s* ____________ to Olivia, and to Oscar and to me."

3 Olivia says, "Things like parkour are easy when you're *c* ____________."

4 Ling says, "When Oscar and I are together, yeah, we have a good *t* ____________."

5 WRITING A really good friend

► SB, p. 45

Think of a really good friend – at school, in your family, in your street, etc. Write why you like this person so much. Write four sentences or ☒ six sentences.

He is She is	always often never	angry. brave. confident. fair. friendly. good fun. funny. honest. kind. mean.

You can use phrases from exercise 4b:
– I think that's really important.
– And we have a good time.

My best friend is ____________

He / She is ____________

____

____

____

____

I can describe what someone looks like.

Erklär-film

6 LANGUAGE Simple past: *yes/no*-questions and short answers

► SB, p. 46

Look at the picture of Oscar's day at the beach. Then answer the questions.

Yes, No,	he she they	did. didn't.

1 Did Oscar go to a big town?
– No, ______

2 Did Ling wear a hat?
– Yes, ______

3 Did they take a bottle of water?
– ______

4 Did Oscar go with his brother Freddie? – ______

5 Did Ling eat an apple? – ______

6 Did Oscar and Ling have a good time? – ______

7 LANGUAGE Did Oscar and Ling do the same things?

► SB, p. 46

a) **Read the sentences and write the verbs 2–4. Then complete the questions.**

> **!**
> I stay**ed** → **Did** you stay?
> **Did** + *Grundform* in questions.

Sentences	Grundform des Verbs	Questions
1 Oscar listened to music.	listen	1 Did Ling listen ______ to music?
2 He played a game or two.	______	2 Did she ______ a game or two?
3 He visited a friend.	______	3 Did she ______ a friend?
4 He texted his dad.	______	4 Did she ______ her dad?

b) **Now read these sentences and write the verbs 6–9. Then complete the questions.**

> **!**
> I **saw** → **Did** you see?
> **Did** + *Grundform* in questions.

Sentences	Grundform des Verbs	Questions
5 Ling went into the sea.	go	5 Did Oscar go ______ into the sea?
6 She swam in the sea.	______	6 Did he ______ in the sea?
7 She bought an ice cream.	______	7 Did he ______ an ice cream?
8 She told a joke or two.	______	8 Did he ______ a joke or two?

8 LANGUAGE Mum's many questions

▸ Digital help ▸ SB, p. 47

When Oscar came home from town, his mum wanted to know ... everything!
Read the dialogue and write the correct question words.
Tipp: Look at Oscar's answers. Then choose the right question word.

how • what • when • where • who • why

Mum Why did you go to town, Oscar?
Oscar I met somebody.
Mum __________ did you meet?
Oscar I met Ling. We went to the cinema.
Mum Oh, __________ film did you watch?
Oscar We watched *Superhero III.* Then we went for a walk.
Mum __________ did you go?
Oscar To the park. And we ate something.
Mum __________ did you leave the cafe?
Oscar At half past five. And then we came home.
Mum __________ did you come home?
Oscar By bus.
Mum __________ did you take the bus? You can walk!
Oscar Oh, Mum! I was tired!

9 LANGUAGE Simple past: questions with question words All about you

Erklärfilm

▸ SB, p. 47

a) **Write the questions with the words in the right order.**

b) **Now answer the questions in full sentences.**

1 *to bed / when / you / did / go / last night / ?*
____
– I went to bed last night at __________

2 *you / to bed / go / why / did / at that time / ?*
____
– I ______ to bed then because __________

3 *for breakfast / you / did / what / this morning / have / ?*
____
– I __________ for breakfast.

4 *did / how / to school / come / you / ?*
____
– I __________

5 *your first lesson / you / have / where / did / ?*
____
– I __________

10 LANGUAGE Four funny questions

▶ Digital help ▶ SB, p. 47

a) Write four funny questions for your partner about last weekend.

Ideas
• see an elephant / …? • have a drink with …? • swim to …?

1 Last weekend, did you *see an elephant* ________________ ? ☐

2 Did you ________________ ? ☐

3 ________________ ? ☐

4 ________________ ? ☐

b) Now ask your partner your questions and your partner answers.
Tick (✓) the box for 'Yes, I did.' and put an ✕ in the box for 'No, I didn't'.

c) Now answer your partner's questions. The partner with more ✕ wins.

11 READING A hero for today

▶ SB, p. 49

a) Read Oscar's article on the next page. Then read the questions and answer with short answers.

1 Did Greta Thunberg save a baby from the sea? ________, *she* ________ ________

2 Did she sit inside an important building? ________ *she* ________

3 Did a lot of people sit with her on the first day? ________ *they* ________

4 Did she talk to people the next day? ________ *she* ________

5 Did lots of people hear her message? ________ *they* ________

b) What about you? Do you think Oscar's hero is a great hero?
Complete sentence one or sentence two.

1 Yes, because ________________

____

2 No, because ________________

____

www.schoolpaper.example.com

My hero – *by Oscar*

My hero is a girl, and people around the world[1] knew her name when she was only 15. What did she do? She didn't do anything exciting or dramatic. She didn't run into the sea and save a baby from the water. She just sat[2] in front of an important building in her home city. She didn't jump up and down or make a loud noise. But it was a Friday, and she didn't go to school.

And that difficult first day she was alone. I think that's very brave. I don't like to be alone for three or four hours – even at home!

But the next day some people asked the girl why she was there. And she said she was there to save our planet. It was a clear message because it was easy to understand. And many people thought, 'Do you know what? She's right!' And soon students in countries around the world went to demonstrations on Fridays and said, 'We must do more for our planet.' In 2019, an amazing number of people took action[3] to save the world – 14 million! And many more people heard her message in the media.

There are still protests today. Everybody remembers the picture of Greta Thunberg sitting alone. Everybody remembers her message. And everybody knows her message is still true.

12 Techno quiz

▸ SB, p. 50

a) **Work with a partner.**

Partner A says these dates to partner B: ***1832, 1852, 1932, 1969, 1995, 2010, 2021, 1975, 2000.***
Then partner B says these dates to partner A: ***1980, 2000, 2010, 1949, 1969, 1999, 1994, 2004, 2014.***

b) **Read the questions and discuss the answers with your partner. Tick (✓) the correct date.**

1	When was the world's first computer?	1832 ☐	1852 ☐	1932 ☐
2	When were there one million computers in the world for the first time?	1980 ☐	2000 ☐	2010 ☐
3	When was the first video film from Mars?	1995 ☐	2010 ☐	2021 ☐
4	When was the world's first message by internet?	1949 ☐	1969 ☐	1999 ☐
5	When was the world's first mobile phone with a camera?	1975 ☐	2000 ☐	2010 ☐
6	When was the world's first smartphone?	1994 ☐	2004 ☐	2014 ☐

14

c) LISTENING **Now listen to the answers. Were you right in part b)?**

[1] **around the world** *weltweit* [2] **sit (simple past: sat)** *sitzen* [3] **take action** *aktiv werden*

I can **ask and answer questions about my hero.**

13 Speaking Weird superheroes

► SB p.50

Partner B: Look at page 87.
Partner A: Stay on this page.

a) Look at your picture of a superhero.
Answer your partner's questions about it.

How many heads does it have?

It has two heads.

b) Now ask questions about your partner's superhero.
And then draw it in the box on the right.

How many	heads noses hands	eyes feet teeth	does it have?

c) Now look at your partner's picture.
Is your picture the same?

14 Clothes for superheroes

► SB, p. 50

a) Look at the letters and write the words.

1 b o t o s — *boots* [E]

2 s o e h s — ______ [ ]

3 c p a e — ______ [ ]

4 d r s e s — ______ [ ]

5 h e e m l t — ______ [ ]

6 s i w m u s i t — ______ [ ]

7 t o r e u r s s — ______ [ ]

8 m s a k — ______ [ ]

b) Now match the words 1–8 with the pictures A–H. Write A–H in the boxes above.

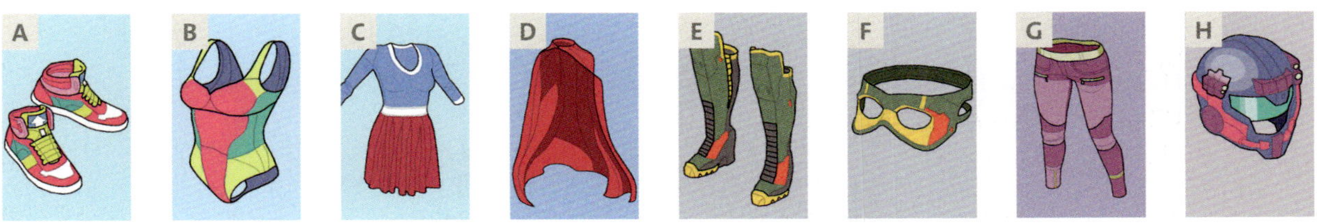

15 Superheroes

▸ SB, p. 51

a) Ello is a superhero. Read his sentences and circle the endings with the right word order.

> **!**
> Word order in English: subject – verb – object

1 I lived on planet Jacus when I was a child / I a child was.

2 I became a superhero when I had an accident / I an accident had.

3 I flew to earth when monsters killed my parents / monsters my parents killed.

4 I was really happy when I on earth arrived / I arrived on earth.

5 Now I help people when they in trouble are / they are in trouble.

b) Complete Xanra's text with the correct words from the box.

became • born • climb • dress • planet • power • run

My name is Xanra and I was (1) __________ on earth, not on a different (2) __________. I (3) __________ a superhero one day when I fell and hurt my head. I'm young, but I'm brave, confident and strong and I use my magic (4) __________ to help people and to save them from horrible people. I can (5) __________ very tall buildings and I can swim and (6) __________ very fast. I wear a red (7) __________, red boots and a red helmet.

c) Complete the network with words from a) and b) and your own ideas.

I'm a superhero
- I am
- I can
- I wear
- I use my power to
- I was born
- I became a superhero when

d) Compare with a partner. Can you add words to your network?

I can write about superheroes.

16 Reading Tell the story

SB, pp. 52–54

Look at the story on pages 52–53 in your book. Answer the questions about the story.

1 What did the four friends and Finn talk about at the start of the story?

They talked ______

2 What do people do in parkour?

They jump ______

3 What was Finn's big mistake?

He said parkour looked easy, but ______

4 How did the friends help Finn? Give four more examples.

They called 999. They ______

______

17 What do you think?

► SB, pp. 52–54

a) **Write what you think.**

1 Why do you think Finn wanted to do what Lily did?

______

2 Do you think the four friends did the right thing? Why (not)?

Yes, because ______

No, because ______

b) **Compare your answers with a partner.**

18 Listening The end of the story

15

► SB, pp. 52–54

a) **Listen to the end of the story and circle the correct answer. Work with a partner.**

		A	B
1	Finn's ankle ...	A hurts a lot.	B doesn't hurt too much now.
2	The four friends say that they ...	A worried about Finn.	B saw Finn in his room.
3	Lily is sorry that she ...	A talked to Finn about parkour.	B showed Finn parkour.
4	Finn says he was stupid because he ...	A didn't listen to Lily.	B worried too much.
5	Zane's jokes ...	A were funny.	B weren't funny.

b) **Now listen again to the end of the story and check your answers.**

I can **understand a story about working in a team.**

19 Singular or plural?

▸ Digital help

Write the plural form of the words. Add *-s* or *-es* only if you must.

1 
brace___

2 
hair___

3 
glass___

4 
trouser___

Are the words singular or plural in your language?

5 
vegetable___

6 
fruit___

7 
rubbish___

8 
clothe___

9 
headphone___

20 Describing people

braces • curly • eyes • face • glasses • long • nose • short • straight

a) **Write the right word from the box under each picture.**

1 
_____ hair

2 
_____ hair

3 
_____ hair

4 
________ hair

5 
____

6 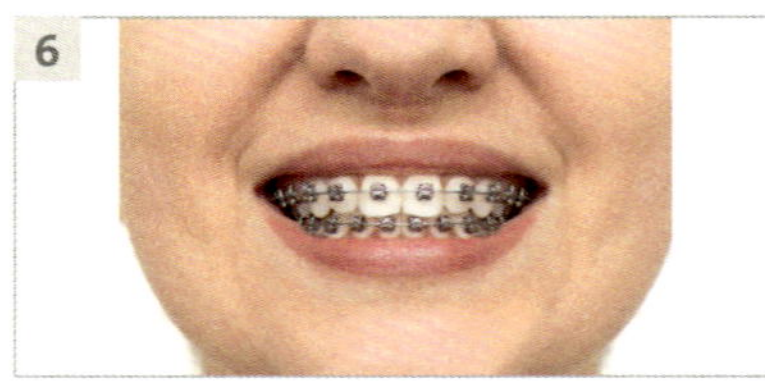
____

7 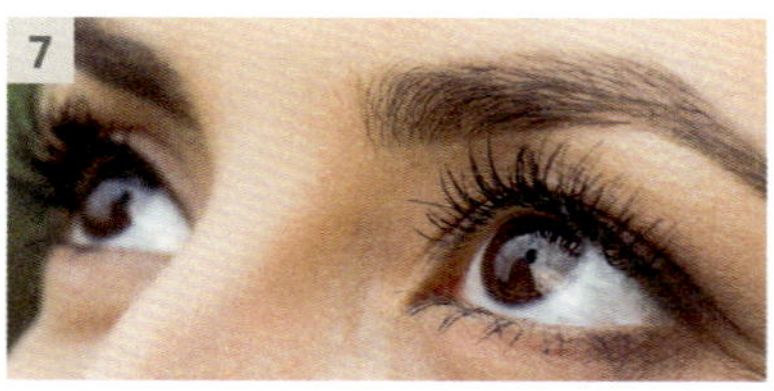
brown ____

8 
a red ____

9 
a happy ____

b) **Look at the picture of Emma. Then write three sentences to describe her and what she's wearing.**

Emma has ____

____

____

21 People

Complete the sentences with the right adjective from the box.

confident • famous • funny • honest • ill • kind • polite • strong

1 Oliver always knows the right thing to do. He's ______________.
2 Erin tells good jokes. She's ______________.
3 What Hassan says is always true. He's ______________.
4 Everybody knows Adele. She's ______________.
5 Julia never forgets to say 'Please' and 'Thank you.' She's ______.
6 Shakila helps people and says nice things to them. She's ______.
7 Jack isn't well. He's ______________.
8 Look at Leah. She's ______________!

22 Small words

a) **Complete the sentences with the right word from the box.**

at • for • from • in • last • like • of • to

1 I often think __________ my friend Aylin in Turkey.
2 We lived next __________ her family in Turkey.
3 But I came here __________ year.
4 I'm happy when I get a text __________ Aylin.
5 We often send messages __________ the evening.
6 Aylin is good __________ listening.
7 I want to be more __________ her.
8 I can't wait __________ July when I can see her again.

b) **Check your answers with a partner.**

23 Speak English well: Sandwich or language?

16 a) **Listen to the words. Can you hear how [tʃ] and [dʒ] are different?**

[tʃ] as in sandwich:	**[dʒ] as in language:**
cheese, teacher, children, chocolate, football match	joke, June, geography, fire engine, page

16 b) **Listen again and repeat the words in a).**

c) **Now say these sentences. Be careful with the sounds in blue.**

1 I like jelly!
2 Don't jump!
3 Are you vegetarian?
4 Did you enjoy your journey?
5 Did you start your new job in July?
6 I'm German. Are you German too?

Jess is playing chess.

My favourite pages in Unit 2 in my book:

Write the page numbers: ______

Four words that are hard to write:

straight ______

______

______

Useful question words:

______

______

______

I can:

Say what people look like: *She has straight* ______

______

Describe a person's personality: *polite,* ______

______

Ask and answer questions in the simple past: *Did you* ______

What did you ______

Say what a hero or superhero does: *she helps people,* ______

______

I have learned:

More clothes words: *dress,* ______

______

How to say dates: I can say: 2022 ☐ 2049 ☐ 1937 ☐ 1484 ☐ 2000 ☐

More parts of the body: *face,* ______

My progress in English:

Write 1–4 in the circles: 1 easy 2 quite easy 3 quite hard 4 hard

Speaking ◯ Writing ◯ Learning new words ◯

Write what you can do to get better: ______

1 Your perfect head student

a) Make a mind map with words and sentences that describe your perfect head student. Write as many ideas as you can. Tip: Look on pages 40–43 if you need ideas.

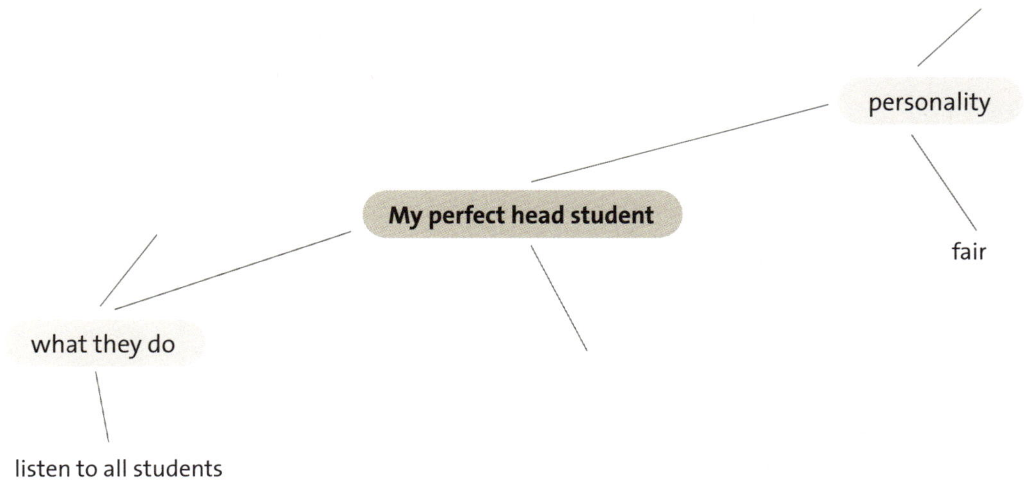

b) Compare with a partner. Did you have the same ideas?

► Check

2 Questions for Greta Thunberg

a) Read the text about Greta Thunberg on page 30 again. Then write some questions to interview her about her life as a child and about what she did in her protest. Use these ideas or your own.

Where did you go to school?
How did you feel when you ...?
Why did you ...?

Where did you

b) Compare your questions with your partner's questions. Choose the four best questions.

c) Now work with another pair and choose the four best questions for the interview.

► Check

1 Tia's friends

a) Write about Tia's friends.
Write the right words from the box.

blond • braces • curly • eyes • glasses • short • straight • worried

1 Sarah has ____________  black hair and she wears ____________ 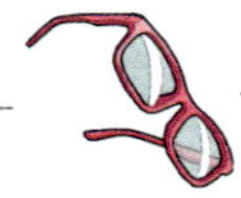.

2 Yuri has ____________ brown hair . He has ____________ 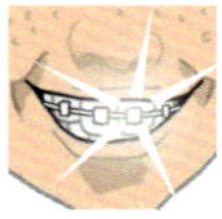.

3 Emily has ____________  brown hair and brown ____________ .

4 George has short ____________  hair and often looks ____________ .

b) Now complete the personality words with: *an / en / in / on (3x) / un*.

1 Emily is k ___ d, happy and often very f ___ ny. I think she's very brave too.

2 Sarah is str ___ g and confid ___ t – sometimes crazy, but always h ___ est.

3 George is sometimes ___ gry, but he's never mean. He's a w ___ derful friend.

Erklär-film

2 A holiday in Spain

Match the questions and answers about a holiday.
Write letters A–H below.

1 ___ 2 ___ 3 ___ 4 ___ 5 ___ 6 ___ 7 ___ 8 ___

1 Where did you go on holiday?
2 Why did you go there?
3 How did you go there?
4 Where did you stay?
5 What did you do there?
6 Did you have a good time?
7 When did you come back?
8 Was the plane late?

A Yes, we did.
B No, it wasn't.
C We went to Spain.
D We went swimming and we visited our friends.
E Because we have friends there.
F Last week.
G In a holiday apartment.
H We went by plane.

► Check

3 Questions, questions, questions

Complete Uncle Tim's boring questions and Tia's short answers: ✓ = yes, ✗ = no.

1 *Did* ______ you *have* ______ breakfast this morning, Tia? *Yes, I did.* ✓
2 ______ your parents ______ to work early? *No, they didn't.* ✗
3 ______ your brother ______ late? ______ ✗
4 ______ your mum *take* ______ you to school? ______ ✓
5 *Was* ______ school hard today? *Yes, it was.* ✓
6 ______ your friends happy to see you? ______ ✓
7 ______ the food in the canteen good? ______ ✓

4 Clothes and things

What are the models wearing? And what do they have? Write the words.

1

useful *b* ______
nice *t* ______

2

cool *g* ______
great *s* ______
beach *b* ______

3

cycling *g* ______
strong *h* ______
black *b* ______

4

long *d* ______
dancing *s* ______

5 Body words

What hurts? Complete the words.

1 my *n e* ______ 	2 my *nk* ______ 	3 my *l g* ______ 
4 my *ea* ______ 	5 my *y* ______ 	6 my *oo* ______ 

▶ Check

Unit 3
Activities and games

1 British pantomimes

► SB, p. 71

These shows are very special. Are the following sentences right (✓) or wrong (✗)?

1 A pantomime is a show for adults only. ☐
2 Pantomimes are full of fun. ☐
3 Pantomimes are often just called "pantos". ☐
4 There are songs and music in pantos. ☐
5 Pantomimes are on in summer. ☐
6 When you watch a pantomime you must be very quiet. ☐
7 The characters in pantomimes sometimes wear funny things. ☐

2 Activity verbs

► SB, p. 71

Write the missing verbs. They are all on pages 70 and 71.

1 H________ fun!
2 Can you c________ Thai food?
3 Hey, come and w________ the show!
4 If you're creative you m________ things.
5 Do you want to s________ a song?
6 You l________ things on a course.

3 Find the partners

► SB, p. 71

Match the blue parts (1–6) with the orange ones (A–F). Draw lines.

1 costs nothing	A boring
2 ride a zip wire	B free
3 not interesting	C delicious
4 really good food	D exciting
5 jokes	E funny

I can talk about family activities.

4 LISTENING Plans for Saturday

17

▶ SB, p. 73

a) **What are the people going to do on Saturday?**
Listen to Oscar and write the letter of the correct picture under the people.

Mum	Freddie and Olivia	Me (Oscar!)	My cousin Amelia	Grandma and grandpa	All of us!
______	______	______	______	______	______

A

B

C

D

E

F

b) **Read sentences 1–6. Then listen again and pick the right option.**

1 Mum is going to leave the house at nine o'clock / ten o'clock.

2 Freddie and Olivia are going to go out with their parents / some friends.

3 Oscar and his team are preparing for a competition / a special meal.

4 Amelia's course is going to be in the morning / in the afternoon.

5 Later grandma and granddad are going to go to the cinema / Oscar's house.

6 Oscar feels excited about what they're going to do in the evening / the next day.

5 Which activities can you do in activity week?

▶ SB, p. 73

Look again at page 72. Then complete the sentences with words from the box.

acting • history • blanket • practise • skills • visit

1 You can learn new photography ____________.

2 You can ____________ a real football stadium.

3 You can knit a toy animal or a ____________.

4 You can learn about Brighton's ____________!

5 You can prepare a show with singing and ____________.

6 You can ____________ karate in the sports hall.

6 Some English-speaking countries

Read the texts and look at the map. Then write the names of the countries.

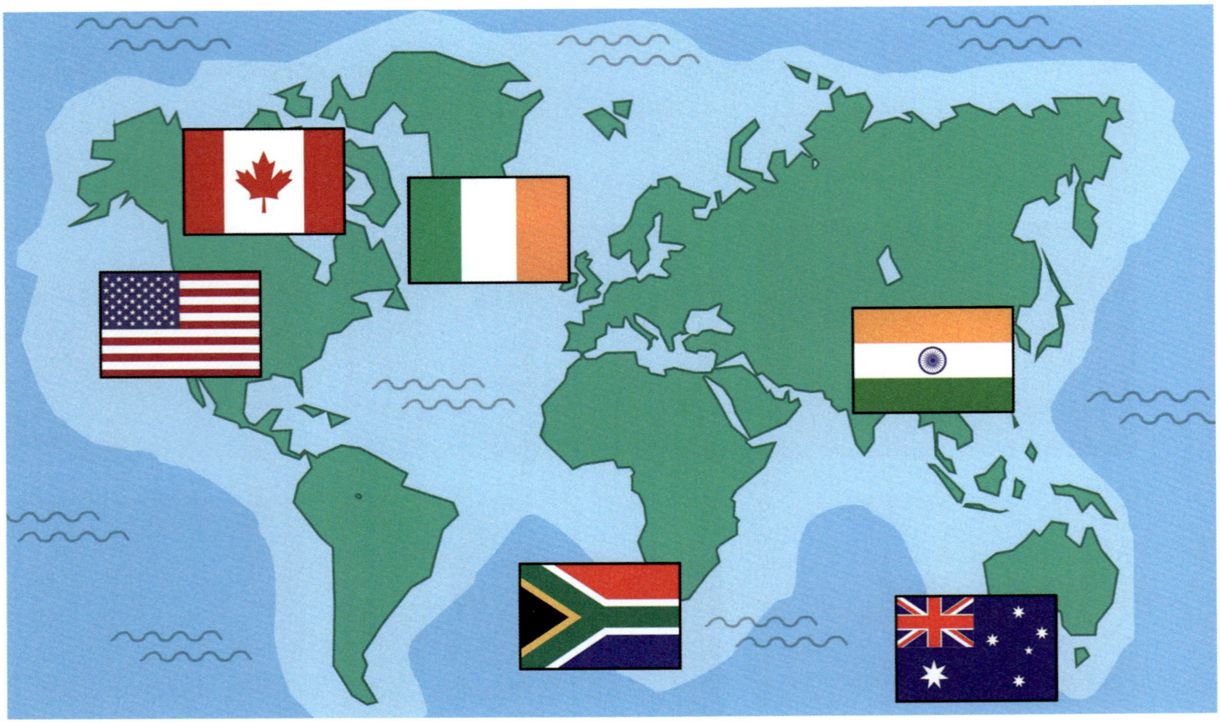

1 This country has more people than any other country in the world. (Yes, more than China!) English is an important language in universities and politics.

This is ________________.

2 English is one of eleven official languages in this African country. The country is famous for its wild animals – from elephants to penguins.

This is ________________.

3 This is the second biggest country in the world. Most people speak English and one province is still called British Columbia (it hasn't been British since 1931).
This is ________________.

4 This is the second biggest country in the southern hemisphere – after Brazil. It has animals that don't live in any other country, for example kangaroos.

This is ________________.

5 This country was a British colony till 1766. English is the official language, but more and more people also speak Spanish.

This is the ________________.

6 This European country, west of Britain, is one of three EU countries where you drive on the left. More than 95 % of the people speak English and nearly 30 % can also speak Irish.
This is ________________.

7 Not fair

► SB, p. 74

Match the questions and answers. Write A–F in the boxes.

1 Are we going to have chips for dinner, Dad?
2 Is mum going to have dinner with us?
3 And what are we going to do after dinner?
4 Are Freddie and Olivia going to watch too?
5 Oh! What are you going to watch?
6 That's not fair! What am I going to do?

A Olivia's favourite film.
B You're going to do your homework, Oscar!
C No, we aren't. We're going to have pasta.
D Well, I'm going to watch a film.
E No, she's going to be home late.
F Yes, they are. They're going to watch with me.

1		2		3		4		5		6	

8 What's the time?

► SB, p. 74

Write the times in words:
quarter to, quarter past or half past.

!
Vorsicht!

half past **ten** = halb **elf**

1 

quarter past three

2 

____

3 

____

4 

____

5 

____

6 

____

7 

____

8 

____

9 

____

I can say at what time activities happen.

9 LANGUAGE Comparatives What can you see?

► Digital help ► SB, p. 77

a) Read the sentences. Circle the correct word: *than* or *as*.

b) Then tick (✓) the correct sentence.

1 In diagram 1
- A is longer than / as B. ☐
- A is as long than / as B. ☐
- B is longer than / as A. ☐

2 In diagram 2
- table A is as big than / as table B. ☐
- table A is bigger than / as table B. ☐
- table B is bigger than / as table A. ☐

3 In diagram 3
- A is as big than / as B. ☐
- A is bigger than / as B. ☐
- B is bigger than / as A. ☐

4 In photo 4
- side B is longer than / as side A. ☐
- side A is longer than / as side B. ☐
- side A is as long than / as side B. ☐

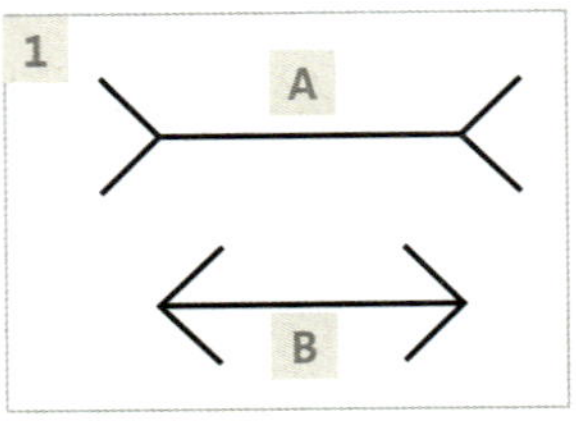

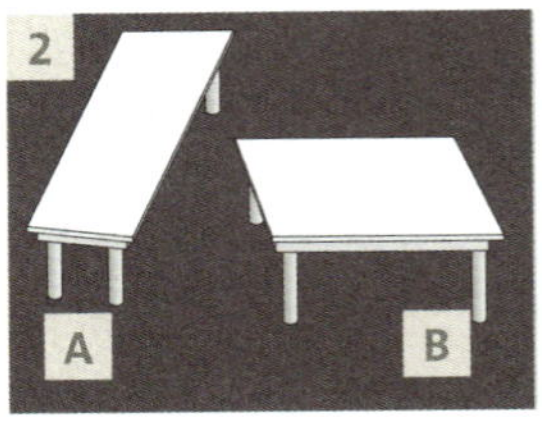

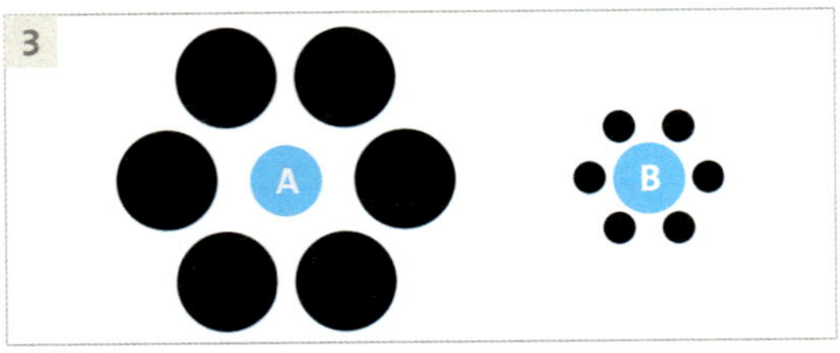

10 Talking about music

► SB, p. 77

a) Look at the jukebox and circle the adjectives that describe music.

b) What kind of music do you like?

I like ______________________

____

____

11 LANGUAGE Comparatives Talking about hobbies

Erklär-film

► SB, p. 77

a) **Write each adjective in the box in the right category.**

bad • ~~cool~~ • creative • easy • energetic • exciting • good • happy • loud • relaxing

two short adjectives like long → longer	**two adjectives end in -y** like busy → busier	**long adjectives** like important → more important	**two adjectives with irregular forms**
cool			

b) **Now write the adjectives in the comparative form.**

I love knitting. It's (1) more relaxing (relaxing) than games. And it's (2) ________ (creative). I knit when I feel sad, and then I feel (3) ________ (happy).

Yes, but dancing is (4) ________ (energetic). OK, it's (5) ________ (loud), but it's (6) ________ (cool) and (7) ________ (exciting) too.

I'm not good with my hands, so for me drawing is hard. And knitting is (8) ________ (bad). Photography is (9) ________ (good). It's much (10) ________ (easy) than knitting!

Erklär-film

12 LANGUAGE Superlatives

► SB, p. 78

The small car, 100 mph, 1990

The sports car, 150 mph, 2016

The big family car, 120 mph, 2021

a) Write the adjectives in the superlative.

1 cheap: the *cheapest* ____________ car   2 good: the ____________ car

3 expensive : the ____________ car

b) Complete sentences 1–6.

1 The sports car is *the cheapest* ____________ (cheap) car. ☐

2 The big family car is ____________ (expensive) car. ☐

3 The smallest car is also ____________ (old) car. ☐

4 The sports car is the ____________ (new) car. ☐

5 The sports car is also the ____________ (fast) car. ☐

6 Which do *you* think is the ____________ (good) car? ____________

c) Now look at the pictures above. Are the sentences right (✓) or wrong (✕)?

13 A mind map about films

► SB, p. 78

Complete the mind map with words from the box.

a crazy boy • a doctor • a famous woman • a great story • a vet • amazing music • an accident • boring • exciting • fast action • love • popular • sad • scary • space

The main character is: ____________

What the film is about: ____________

Films

The film is ____________

The film has ____________

I can compare music, shows and films.

14 Places in town

► SB, p. 81

a) Read the sentences and look at the pictures. Then write the right eight words in the puzzle.

1 A place where you can see a pantomime.
2 This is where trains stop.
3 A place with lots and lots of trees.
8 A place where you can borrow books.

4

5

6

7

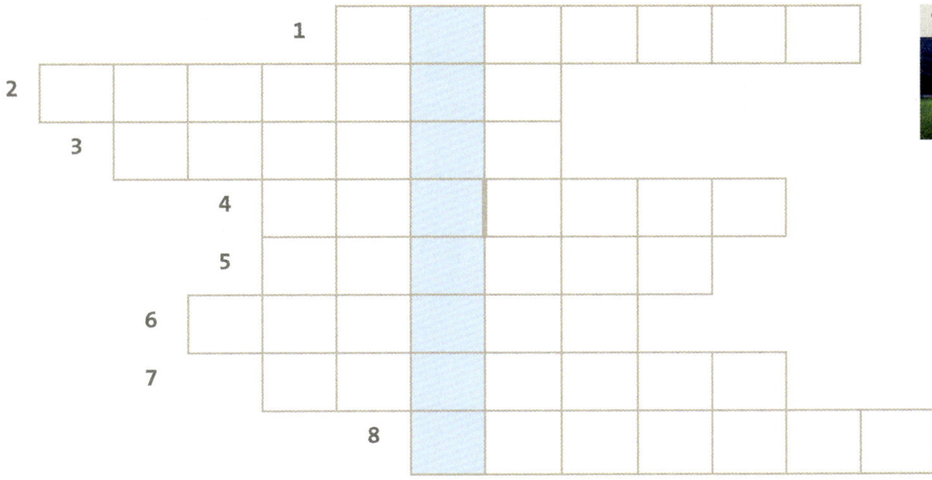

b) Write a definition for the place in blue.

It's the place where you must go if ______________________________

15 Directions

► SB, p. 81

Match the phrases and the pictures.

1 Go through the forest.
2 Turn left.
3 Go straight on.
4 Go past some shops.
5 Turn right.
6 Go across the bridge.
7 Go up the street.
8 Go down the road.

1	2	3	4
5	6	7	8

A

B

C

D

E
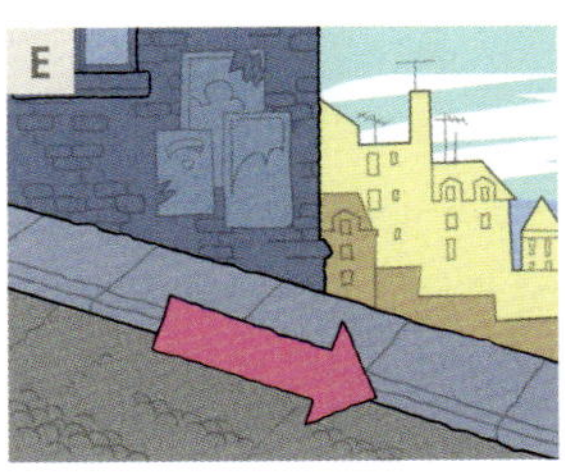
F

G

H

16 In town

▶ SB, p. 81

18 **a)** LISTENING **Listen to the directions. You always start from "Start". Where do the directions take you to?**

1 ____________ 2 ____________ 3 ____________ 4 ____________

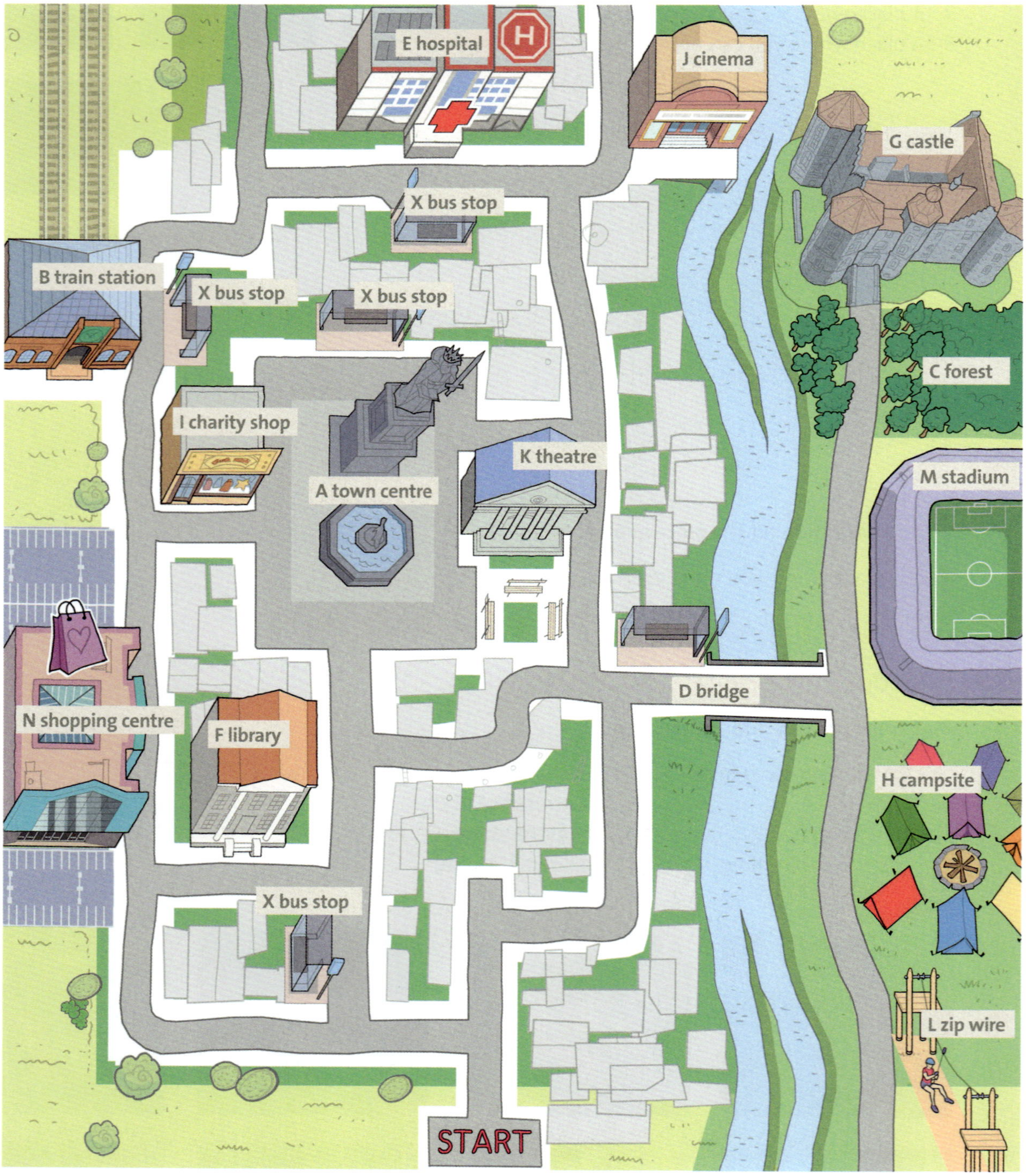

b) SPEAKING **Work with a partner.**

- Give your partner directions to a place in town, but don't say which place it is.
- Your partner listens and follows on the map. Does your partner arrive at the correct place?
- Then swap roles.

I can give directions.

17 VIEWING Wrong information

► SB, p. 85

a) **Read sentences 1–5. Circle the correct information in each sentence.**

Part 1 (00:30 to 01:11)

1 Daisy asks her friends to do gardening with her this evening / this week.

2 Gloria doesn't want to do gardening with Daisy because she has photography club / a sewing project.

Part 2 (01:12 to 01:37)

3 When they meet at the street dance club, Emir / Joe teaches the others how to dance.

Parts 3 and 4 (01:38 to 05:08)

4 When they begin dancing, Emir finds it really easy / hard.

5 Gloria wins / doesn't win a prize.

b) **Now watch the film and check your answers with a partner**

18 VIEWING What's the missing word?

► SB, p. 85

Watch the video and write the missing words.

Part 1 (00:30 to 01:11)

1 Joe: 'Come with me after school tomorrow! And I can teach you some new th__________.'

Part 2 (01:12 to 01:37)

2 Joe: 'Don't worry, we'll go s__________.'

3 Joe: 'The person who dances well and learns the most will w__________.'

Part 3 and 4 (01:38 to 05:08)

4 Joe: 'That's OK, Emir. Let's try a__________.'

5 Gloria: 'That was so much fun. Let's do some m__________!'

19 And you?

► SB, p. 85

What do you think? Write your answer. Useful words: *because, fun, scary, good at it, do what you like, ...*

Do you like freestyle dancing? Why (not)?

____

because ____________________________________.

20 Which way do you go?

Look at the pictures. Complete the sentences.

1 

a ss

2 

p t

3 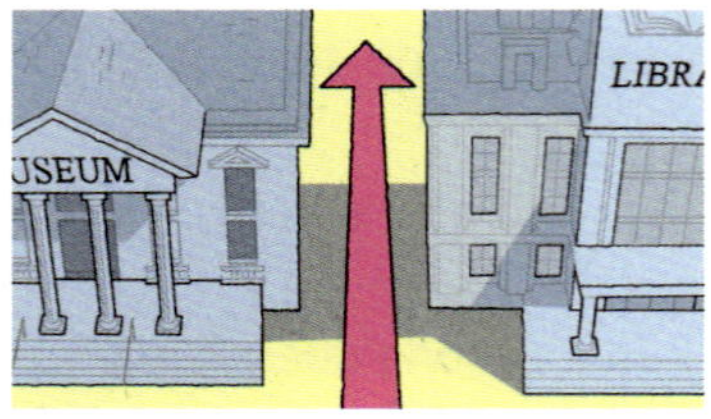

b een

4 

r

5 

l

6 

str t o

21 The right order

Choose the right words in blue and write the six sentences.

1 I spent	a trophy	in France on a photography course.
2 Every day I practised	a photo of a group	skills.
3 I also prepared	a week	on the last day.
4 Our teacher told us	for a competition	of the competition.
5 On the last day I took	the rules	of goats.
6 And our teacher gave me	my photography	for my photo.

1 I spent

2 Every day

3

4

5 On the last day

6 And

22 Words in Unit 3

Write the words in the puzzle. You can work with a partner.

1 Animals with six legs.
2 In a house, you use the ... to go up to the bedrooms.
2 ↓ *(down)* Where the sun, moon and planets are.
3 ↓ *(down)* These tell you how to play a game.
4 You have this when your head hurts.
5 ↓ *(down)* You use it to take photos.
6 Don't turn left, don't turn right, go ... *(2 words)*
7 It gives you the dates in a year.
7 ↓ *(down)* simple past of *come*
8 In a film this person works secretly for a country.
9 ↓ *(down)* A farm animal
10 ↓ *(down)* It's big and it stands in a forest or garden.
11 When you are next to things on two sides, you are ... them.

23 SPEAKING Speak English well: How do you say EA?

a) **How do you say EA in the words in the box? Write them in the correct pronunciation[1] categories.**

beach • break • ~~bread~~ • dead • easy • ~~great~~ • head • ~~meal~~ • meat • season • weather

1 [iː] as in **meal**: meal,

2 [eɪ] as in great: great,

3 [e] as in **bread**: bread,

19

b) **Now listen to the words. Were your answers in part a) right?**

[1] **pronunciation** *Aussprache*

My favourite topic in Unit 3 in my book: ____________________

Different kinds of music:

rap, ____________________

____

____

What I know about British pantomimes:

great shows, ____________________

____

____

I can:

Tell the time:  *It's* ______ *three.*

 ____________________

 ____________________

Make plans for the weekend: *I'm going to* ____________________

____

I can compare people and things:

tall: ______ *than / the* ______

exciting: ______ *than / the* ______

good: ______ *than / the* ______

bad: ______ *than / the* ______

Give directions: *Turn* ____________________

My progress[1] in English:

What's easy or difficult when I write English?

Write 1–4 in the boxes: 1 easy 2 quite easy 3 quite hard 4 hard

having good ideas ☐ thinking of the right word ☐ spelling ☐ grammar ☐

[1] **progress** *Fortschritt*

1 Your plan for a perfect Saturday

a) READING **Read Oscar's plan for a perfect Saturday.**

In the morning *I stay in bed till half past ten.*
For lunch *I have sausages, eggs and chips.*
After lunch *I play football with my friends.*
And then we eat jelly and custard in the park!
In the evening *I go to a show at the theatre.*

b) WRITING **Now write a plan for your perfect Saturday. What do you do?**

In the morning *I* ______________________

For lunch ______________________

After lunch ______________________

____

In the evening ______________________

c) **Compare your plan with a partner. Did you have the same kinds of ideas?**

2 A times quiz

Read the sentences and write the times. Use *quarter* and *half*, and write the times in words.

1 I arrived in Brighton 30 minutes ago, at 10.00 a.m.

What's the time now? It's *half past ten.*

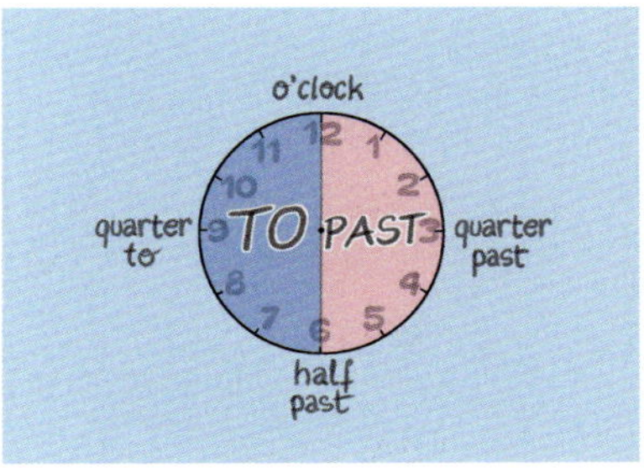

2 We're in our seats, 15 minutes before the show begins at 7.00.

What's the time now? It's ______________________

3 I want to meet my friend Hamid at 2.45. That's in 30 minutes.

What's the time now? It's ______________________

4 My sister went to the Family Arts Centre at four o'clock. That was 45 minutes ago.

What's the time now? It's ______________________ ► Check

1 The time

What time is it? Write the times in words, not numbers.

1 02:00 2 05:15 3 08:30 4 10:45

1 It's *t* ___ *o'* ___________ 2 It's *q* ___ *p* ___ *f* ___________

3 It's *h* ___ *p* ___ *e* ___________ 4 It's *q* ___ *t* ___ *e* ___________

2 No school tomorrow

Complete the sentences.

Remember:

I'm	I'm not	going to
She's	She isn't	
They're	They aren't	

Olivia *I'm not going to be* ___________ at school tomorrow. (I / not / be)

Karim Oh? What ___ *you* ___ going to ___________? (you / do)

Olivia *Ms Jones is* ___ going to ___________ us to a museum in York. (Ms Jones / take)

Karim Oh, sounds cool. ___________ going to ___________ there all day? (you / be)

Olivia I think so. ___________ going to ___________ lunch in a park. (we / have)

And ___________ going to ___________ back in time for the last lesson. (we / not / be)

3 In the country

Look at the picture and write the words.

1 *b* _ _ _ _ _

2 *r* _ _ _ _

3 *f* _ _ _ _ _

4 *m* _ _ _ _ _ _ _

5 *c* _ _ _ _ _ _ _

6 *r* _ _ _ _ _ _

► Check

Erklär-film

4 Which show?

▶ Digital help

a) **Tia and her friends Seb and Kim are talking about three shows. Circle the correct form of the adjective: comparative or superlative.**

The Star Cinema is showing
THE BLUE FOREST
'The best film of the year!'
£8.50

— FAMILY PANTO —
CINDERELLA
at the
Grand Theatre
£12.99

Live concert
Best
DANCE MUSIC
from Ireland
In the City Hall
£15 – £35

Tia I think the film looks more interesting / most interesting than the panto.

Kim Really? I like funny things, and I think the panto is funnier / funniest than the film.

Seb I think the concert is better / the best of all.

Tia Maybe, but the film is cheaper / cheapest than the concert.

Kim Yes, that's true. The film is cheaper / the cheapest of all three.

Tia And the concert is more expensive / the most expensive of all!

Seb Yes, but a concert is more relaxing / most relaxing than a panto.

Kim But a panto is more fun. Films are often scarier / scariest than pantos.

Tia I don't agree. I think that films are better / best than pantos.

I think pantos are stupid. They are my worse / worst idea of an evening out!

Kim Well, OK then. Let's go to the film. Is that OK with you too, Seb?

Seb Fine with me.

b) **Now write the adjectives from part a) in the correct part of the table.**

1 comparative		
–er than	more ... than	*good* changes to:
________ than	*more interesting* ________ than	________ than
________ than	________ than	
________ than		
2 superlative		
the -est	the most ...	*good* and *bad* change to:
the ________	the ________	the ________
		the ________

▶ Check

Unit 4
Celebrate!

1 Pictures of celebrations

► SB, p. 99

a) **Look again at pictures A, B, C, D on** pages 98 and 99 **in your book. In which pictures can you see 1–6?**

1 fun things to wear ____________ 2 vegetables ____________ 3 nice things to eat ____________

4 pink, yellow and red in the sky ____________ 5 two big eyes ____________

6 things that make a loud noise ____________

b) **Write the correct words from the box under the pictures.**

A

____

B

____

C

____

bonfire • candles • carnival • fireworks • food • presents

D

____

E

____

F

____

2 One after the other

► SB, p. 99

Write the words in blue in the correct order.

1 spring, ______ *autumn* ______ (winter, autumn, summer)

2 twenty, ____________ (forty, thirty, fifty)

3 March, ____________ (June, April, May)

4 morning, ____________ (night, evening, afternoon)

5 Halloween, ____________ (Easter, New Year's Day, Christmas)

I can **talk about celebrations.**

Erklär-film

3 LANGUAGE Ling's breakfast, lunch and dinner *some* and *any*

► SB, p. 101

a) **Write the right word: *some* or *any*.**

For breakfast I like to eat (1) ________ toast with jam. I don't usually have (2) ________ yoghurt. But on Sunday dad makes breakfast and we have (3) ________ eggs and (4) ________ vegetarian sausages. I'm vegetarian: I eat fish, but I don't eat (5) ________ meat. So for lunch I like to eat (6) ________ salad or (7) ________ rice with a nice curry. In the evening we have (8) ________ fish and chips, or sometimes (9) ________ pasta with a cheese sauce and (10) ________ vegetables. But I don't have (11) ________ tomatoes, because I don't like tomatoes.

b) **Does Ling eat this? Tick (✓) if yes, put a cross (✗) if no.**

breakfast		lunch		dinner	
1  ☐	2  ☐	3  ☐	4  ☐	5  ☐	6  ☐

4 A picnic with your partner

► SB, p. 101

a) **Partner B: Look at page 87.**
Partner A: Say the six things that you need for a picnic and listen to your partner. Put a tick (✓) if your partner has it. Put an (✗) if not.

eggs	☐	bread	☐
strawberries	☐	tomatoes	☐
lemonade	☐	salad	☐

We need some …

b) **Now look at what you have. Then listen to your partner and answer.**

No problem, I have some …

Sorry, I don't have any …

 ✓  ✓  ✗  ✗  ✓  ✓

c) **Now write what you and your partner still need.**

We still need *some ham, some* ____________________

5 LANGUAGE *a little, a few* Three recipes

► SB, p. 102

Now look at the pictures and complete the recipes with *a little* and *a few*.

1 
2 
3 

1 For a carrot cake we need two eggs, __________ flour and __________ sugar. We also need __________ butter and of course __________ carrots!

2 For a trifle we need some jelly, some fruit, __________ cream and __________ milk.

3 For mattar paneer[1] we need some tomato sauce, __________ peas, an onion and __________ other vegetables.

!
Singular nouns:
a little bread
Plural nouns:
a few sweets

6 LISTENING Four invitations to a meal

20

► SB, p. 102

Listen to four invitations. Circle the right information in the table.

	Day / Time	Meal	Dessert
1	Friday A 6 pm B 6.30 pm	A chicken B lamb with potatoes and vegetables	A ice cream B yoghurt and fruit
2	Monday A 5–6 pm B 6–7 pm	Pasta with A tomato sauce B curry sauce	A trifle B fruit salad
3	Saturday A lunch B dinner	Sausages with A chips B rice	A melon B pancakes
4	After school on A Tuesday B Thursday	A vegetable soup B meat and vegetables	A cake B biscuits

[1] **mattar paneer** Mattar Paneer *(nordindisches Gericht)*

I can describe a special meal.

7 Sunita is getting ready for the wedding

► SB, p. 104–105

Look again at pages 104 and 105 in your book. Then read the sentences below and say if they are right (✓) or wrong (✗).

1 Sunita has thought of some nice stories. ☐
2 She has found photos of her mum and Ben. ☐
3 She has made the slide show. ☐
4 She has found some good music. ☐
5 She has practised the presentation. ☐
6 She has invited some friends. ☐
7 She has bought a present for Ben. ☐
8 She has made a card. ☐

8 SPEAKING Game in class

► Digital help ► SB, p. 105

When the game starts, ask a student in class a question.
If he/she answers 'No, I haven't.', ask a different question.
If he/she answers 'Yes, I have.', write the student's name – and swap roles.
When both partners have finished, go to a different student and ask more questions.
You win if you are the first person with all 9 names or if you have the most names after 10 minutes.

Have you ever …?

Yes, I have.

No, I haven't

1 Have you ever travelled to Italy? Yes? Name: ______	2 Have you ever made a funny costume? Yes? Name: ______	3 Have you ever eaten fish and chips? Yes? Name: ______
4 Have you ever seen a famous film or music star? Yes? Name: ______	5 Have you ever bought a cycling helmet? Yes? Name: ______	6 Have you ever lived in a country outside Germany? Yes? Name: ______
7 Have you ever stayed in bed till 12 o'clock? Yes? Name: ______	8 Have you ever played table tennis? Yes? Name: ______	9 Have you ever had a night in hospital? Yes? Name: ______

9 Oscar's birthday

► SB, p. 105

Oscar is having a great birthday. Complete Oscar's sentences with words from the box.

bought • got • had • given • made • thought

1 Look! Olivia has ________________ an amazing birthday cake.

2 And Freddie has ________________ a great present.

3 Mum and dad have ________________ some great ideas for party games.

4 And I've ________________ some nice winter socks from grandma.

5 And Ling, you have ________________ of so many things!

6 You have all ________________ me a perfect day. Thank you for everything!

10 Crossword

► SB, p. 105

Write the right form of the verbs for the present perfect.

1 Dad has (give) me a nice present!

2 I haven't (see) my present yet.

3 Have you ever (swim) in the sea?

4 Or have you ever (win) a competition?

5 My parents haven't (meet) my friend Noah

6 It's late, and we haven't (eat) yet.

7 Have you (think) of a good game?

8 We have never (be) to Spain.

9 But my friends in Spain have often (come) to us!

10 Tim is looking for me. But he hasn't (find) me.

11 Have you (buy) something nice for lunch?

12 No, but I've (make) a nice cake.

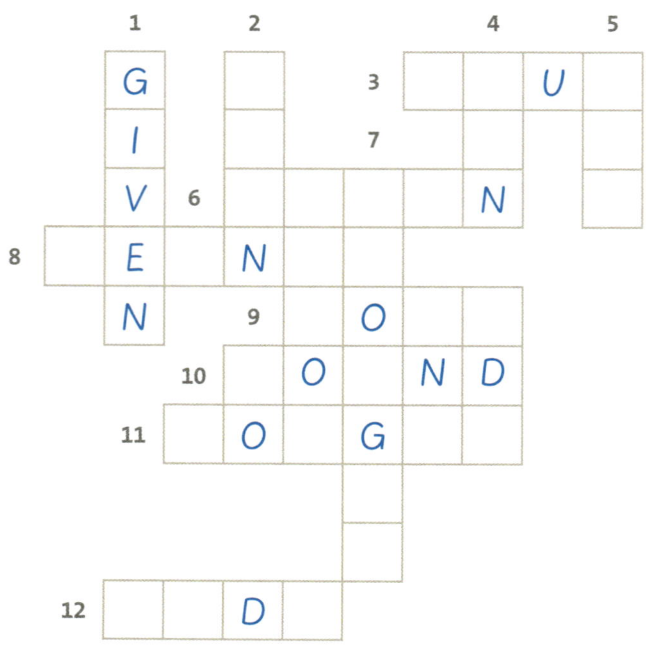

11 Helping at home

► SB, p. 106

a) What do you have to do at home?
Write the verbs.

Do you need help? The verbs are on page 106 in your book.

I have to

g							shopping.
s							the table.
t							my room.
m							my bed.
h							with the cooking.
c							the bathroom.
v							the living room.
t				o			the rubbish. *(two words)*.

b) Oscar's dad is telling Oscar what he has to do – but the last words in the sentences are wrong.
Write the correct words at the end of the sentences.

1 Please vacuum the ~~rubbish~~. ________________!

2 And set the ~~bathroom~~. ________________

3 I want to go shopping so please can you tidy your ~~bed~~? ________________

4 And please take out the ~~living room~~. ________________

5 And can you please make your ~~room~~? ________________

6 Then I will clean the ~~table~~. ________________

c) Now write about three things you have to do at home and three things you don't have to do.

1 I have to ____.

2 I ____.

3 ____.

1 I don't have to ____.

2 I ____.

3 ____.

12 At home

► SB, p. 106

Oscar's parents are out. They have written a list of things for Oscar to do or not to do.

a) **Match instructions 1–9 with pictures A–I.**

1 H 2 ___ 3 ___ 4 ___ 5 ___ 6 ___ 7 ___ 8 ___ 9 ___

Things to do:
1 Make your bed
2 vacuum the living room
3 Take out the rubbish
4 Tidy your room

Things you can do if you want to:
5 go shopping
6 cook the evening meal
7 clean the bathroom

Things NOT to do:
8 use a lot of water
9 make a lot of noise

A

B

C

D

E

F

G

H

I

b) **What does Oscar say?**
Complete his sentences with words from the box.

have to (2x) • don't have to (2x) • ~~mustn't~~ (2x)

!
I have to do it. = Ich muss es tun.
I don't have to do it. = Ich brauche es nicht zu tun.
I mustn't do it. = Ich darf es nicht tun.

1 I mustn't ______ use a lot of water.

2 I ______ make my bed, but

I ______ go shopping.

3 I ______ clean the bathroom, but I ______ vacuum the living room.

4 I ______ make a lot of noise.

c) **And you? Complete three sentences about yourself.**

1 At home I have to ______

2 I don't have to ______

3 But I mustn't ______

I can talk about chores at home.

13 Oscar's train ticket

▶ SB, p. 109

a) Circle the correct word.

b) Complete the sentences with *anything, everything, everybody, everywhere, something.*

c) Act out the scene in a group of three.

14 LISTENING A dangerous party

▸ SB, p. 109

21 **a) Listen to Ling's story and answer the questions.**

1 On what date was the Guy Fawkes party? ________ November.

2 Who had an accident? ________

3 What was important in the story? Tick (✓) the right box.

A

☐

B

☐

C

☐

D

☐

21 **b) Now listen again and tick (✓) the correct answer A–C.**

1 Where did the party start?
A Inside. ☐
B Outside. ☐
C At Ling's school. ☐

2 It was cold, so Ling ...
A wore warm clothes. ☐
B stayed inside. ☐
C went home early. ☐

3 Danielle asked people to move back so that ...
A everyone could see the fireworks. ☐
B everyone could get sausages. ☐
C they weren't too near the fireworks. ☐

4 When everyone went inside, ...
A there was a big meal. ☐
B the house was hot and full. ☐
C everyone was really cold. ☐

5 How did Oscar save Ling? He ...
A told her to move away. ☐
B phoned for a fire engine. ☐
C went to find water. ☐

6 At the end of the story, Oscar ...
A was a bit scared. ☐
B was angry with Danielle. ☐
C angry with Ling. ☐

c) What do YOU think?

1 What was dangerous in the house? ____________________

2 Was Danielle careful? ____________________

I can **talk about family celebrations.**

15 READING Tell the story

▶ SB, pp. 110–112

Put the sentences in the right order. Write 2–9 in the boxes.

☐	A	Two men take the bikes.
☐	B	Willow shows Ben the wedding bikes.
☐	C	Ben goes to his wedding in slippers.
1	D	Ben gets up and puts on his suit and tie.
☐	E	Meera laughs when she sees Ben in his slippers.
☐	I	Ben is worried that Meera isn't going to be happy.
☐	F	Ben and Willow run down the stairs and out into the street.
☐	G	The door of Ben and Willow's house closes.
☐	H	Ben can't get his phone or his money because they're in the house.

16 MEDIATION Help a friend

▶ Digital help ▶ SB, pp. 110–112

Eine Freundin stellt dir Fragen zu Ben und Meeras Hochzeit. Beantworte sie.

1 Was war Sunitas große Angst am Hochzeitstag? ____________________

2 Wie geht es Meera damit? ____________________

3 Wie haben Sunita und Willow vor der Hochzeit geholfen? ____________________

____

4 Warum zog Ben seine Schuhe nicht an? ____________________

____

5 Warum konnte Ben hinterher seine Schuhe nicht anziehen? ____________________

____

☒ 17 STORY What do *you* think?

▶ SB, p. 110–112

What do *you* think: Are Ben and Meera good partners?
Write *Yes* or *No* and give your reason(s).

____

I can talk about different cultures in my life. ✓

18 Ramadan and Eid al-Fitr

What do people usually do? Use the verbs from the box.

Tip: Look again at page 100.

celebrate • eat • get • give • pray • thank

1 Many people don't ______________ anything during the day.

2 They ______________ the end of Ramadan with a big meal.

3 They ______________ to Allah and ______________ him for all good things.

4 They ______________ money to charity.

5 Children often ______________ presents from their parents and grandparents.

19 Food and drinks

▸ Digital help

a) **Look at the pictures and write the nine words in the puzzle.**

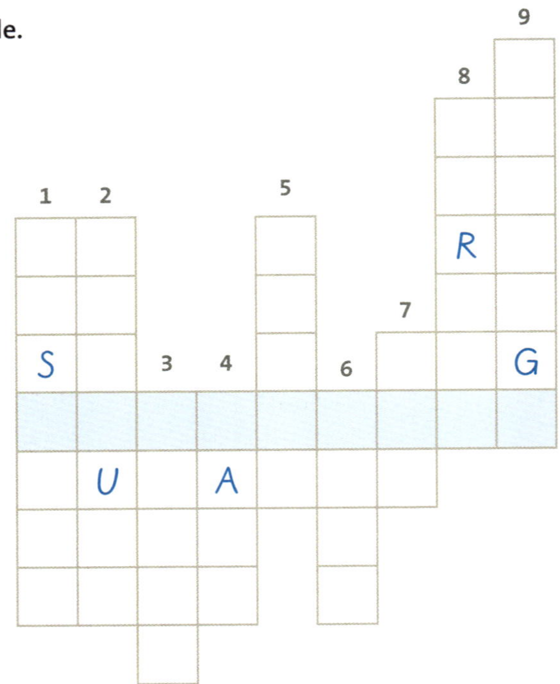

b) **What food word ...**

1 is the word in blue? ______________ 2 can you write with the letters in blue? ______________

c) **Write three ...**

1 foods you can make from milk: y o __ __ __ __ __ __ __, c r __ __ __ __, c h __ __ __ __ __

2 kinds of fruit: a p __ __ __ __, s t r __ __ b __ __ __ __ __ __ s, m e __ __ __ __

3 things you need to make a cake: b u __ __ __ __ __ __, e g __ __, f l __ __ __ r

20 Words for how you feel

Write the adjectives on the right next to the correct meanings (1–7).

This is how you feel when ...

1 you have no friends: *lonely*

2 you are not well and have to stay in bed: ______

3 it's your birthday the next day: ______

4 you know everything will be OK: ______

5 you have a difficult exam the next day: ______

6 you feel really bad: ______

7 you haven't eaten for a long time: ______

confident · excited · hungry · ill · lonely · nervous · terrible

21 Things to wear

Write the words.

1 

s ______

2 

s ______

3 

s ______

4 

t ______

22 SPEAKING Speak English well: When you're happy about something

22 **a) Oscar is having dinner at Ling's house. Listen to his sentences.**

Can you hear it? To sound polite and enthusiastic[1] the intonation goes **up** in the important words of the sentence.

1 I'm REALLY HAPPY to be here.

2 It's so KIND of you!

3 The food is REALLY nice. THANK you.

4 This is an am-A-zing dessert!

5 That was a fan-TAS-tic meal. THANK you.

23 **b) Listen and repeat the sentences in a). Be as polite and enthusiastic as you can!**

[1] **enthusiastic** *begeistert*

The big event in Unit 4 in my book: ____________________

Things for a celebration:

good food, ____________________

____

____

What I know about Eid al-Fitr:

____

____

I remember:

words for food and drinks: ____________________

how to say how much: *a little milk, a few* ____________________

3 chores: *tidy my room,* ____________________

____

I can write full sentences with:

some and *any*: ____________________

____

questions and answers with *ever*: ____________________

My progress[1] in English:

☐ very good ☐ quite good

☐ slower than I want!

[1] **progress** *Fortschritt*

1 Bank holidays in England

a) Use the internet and list the bank holidays in England.

New Year's Day, ______________________

____

____

____

____

- In Britain the days when people get a holiday and don't go to work are called **bank holidays**.
- There are more bank holidays in Scotland and Northern Ireland than in England.
- If a bank holiday is on a Saturday or Sunday, then the next Monday becomes a bank holiday (so the bank holiday isn't 'lost').

b) Now think of the bank holidays where you live.
Who has more bank holidays: people in England or people where you live?

______________________ ▸ Check

2 Celebrations

a) Read the sentences about Ramadan in Zane's family. Then write the correct words in the sentences.

about | because | between | but | during | for | from | in | of | to

(1) ________ Ramadan Zane's dad doesn't eat (2) ________ early morning and late evening. He works (3) ________ a cafe, so of course it's hard (4) ________ him. (5) ________ he fasts (6) ________ it is important to him. The rest (7) ________ the family doesn't fast. Eid al-Fitr isn't just (8) ________ coming together and celebrating. Zane's parents give money (9) ________ charity and Zane often gets presents (10) ________ his grandparents.

▸ Check

b) Now think of your favourite meal.
Write a shopping list for it.

▸ Digital help

My favourite meal is: ______________________

____

1 Food words

a) Write the different sorts of meat.

1 
l ______

2 
p ______

3 
c ______

4 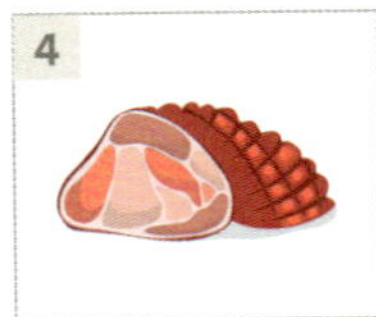
h ______

5 
s ______

b) Now write theses food words.

1 
a few ______

2 
a bottle of ______

3 
a little ______

4 
some ______

5 
three ______

6 
a packet of ______

Erklär-film

2 How much?

Mum is asking Callum to buy a few things in the shop. Complete the text with *some* or *any*.

Can you go to the shop for me, please, Callum? We need
(1) ______ bread and (2) ______ baked beans.
And, wait a moment ... we don't need (3) ______ cheese,
but could you get me (4) ______ butter, please?
And, why not, buy (5) ______ biscuits.
But don't get (6) ______ cake – I'm going to make a cake tomorrow.
Oh yes, get (7) ______ sugar for the cake.
But we don't need (8) ______ flour.

► Check

3 Chores

Look at pictures 1–8. Then complete sentences 1–8 with words from both boxes.

clean • go • help • ~~make~~ • set • take out • tidy • vacuum

my bed • my room • shopping • the bathroom • the living room • the rubbish • the table • with the cooking

I have to (1) *make* ______, but I don't have to (2) ______.

My brother has to (3) ______.

And we all have to (4) ______.

My brother doesn't have to (5) ______.

Mum doesn't have to (6) ______.

I have to (7) ______, but I don't have to (8) ______.

4 My birthday party

Circle the right word.

1 I invited all my family and friends to my party – I didn't forget anybody / everybody.

2 There was a lot to eat and drink and everybody / anybody was happy.

3 The food was good, the cake was good – everywhere / everything was perfect!

4 Then, when we finished eating, something / somebody started to sing a song.

5 Then everybody / anybody sang. I thought it was fun, but ...

6 ... our cat didn't like the singing. He ran away and I couldn't find him everywhere / anywhere!

► Check

Unit 5
Getting ready for the future

1 Looking at the pictures

▸ SB, p. 129

Look at the pictures on pages 128 and 129 in your book. Then write the letter of the right picture A–G. You won't need all the pictures.

a) **The person in the picture is working ...**

1 in an office. ___ 2 in a kitchen. ___ 3 in a hospital. ___ 4 outside. ___

b) **The person in the picture ...**

1 is working at a computer. ___ 2 is wearing a helmet. ___ 3 is wearing red trousers. ___

4 is working on a car. ___ 5 is working with food. ___ 6 is cutting hair. ___

7 is wearing gloves. ___ 8 is working in front of a mirror. ___

2 Lots of different jobs

▸ SB, p. 129

Complete the sentences with words from the box.

artist • cook • firefighter • hairdresser • mechanic • nurse • plumber • programmer

Remember to use **a** or **an** with jobs:
I'm **a** plumber. *Ich bin Klempner/in.*
She's **an** acrobat. *Sie ist Akrobatin.*

1 *I fight fires.* I'm a ______________

2 *I prepare meals.* I'm ______________

3 *I fix showers, baths and toilets.* ______________

4 *I work on cars when they don't work.* ______________

5 *I look after people.* ______________

6 *I make new computer programs.* ______________

7 *I cut people's hair.* ______________

8 *I paint, draw or make other forms of art.* ______________

I can **talk about jobs.**

3 The world of work

► SB, p. 131

a) **Complete the mind map with words from the box – and use your own ideas too** 😊

animals • a business owner • computers • a gamer • a hospital • an office • old people • play football • my own boss • program computers • a hotel • a school • teach • use my English • work outside • a vet

The world of work

- I want to be ....
- I want to work in ...
- I want to work with ...
- I want to ...

b) **Many jobs end in *-er*. Write the jobs.**

1 I swim – I'm a swimmer.

2 I teach – I'm a __________.

3 I clean rooms – I'm a __________.

4 I design clothes – I'm clothes __________.

5 I read the news on TV – I'm a news __________.

6 I play basketball – I'm a basketball __________.

4 LISTENING Different dreams

24

► SB, p. 131

a) **Look at the jobs A–F. Then listen to four teenagers and match them with a job. Write the right letter A–F next to the name. You don't need all the jobs.**

b) **Listen again and write why they chose this job.**

	Name	Job	Why?
1	Muhammad	___	loves making drawings of __________.
2	Isla	___	is interested in[1] __________.
3	Freya	___	wants to really know all about __________.
4	Archie	___	wants to work with other __________.

A vet
B programmer
C plumber
D architect
E nurse
F mechanic

c) **Now check your answers with a partner.**

Muhammad wants to be ... because ... | *Yes, that's right.* | *No, that's wrong. He wants to be ...*

[1] **be interested in** *sich für etwas interessieren*

5 LANGUAGE Will-future The weather tomorrow

Erklär-film

► SB, p. 132

Look at the online weather forecast[1] for York tomorrow. Then circle *will* or *won't* in the sentences.

1 It says it will / won't be sunny today.
2 It says it will / won't rain today.
3 But it will / won't be windy.
4 It says it will / won't snow today.
5 It will / won't be warm today.
6 It will / won't be cold today.

6 LANGUAGE Will-future Oscar and Ling

► Digital help ► SB, p. 132

What will Oscar and Ling do on Saturday? Write sentences with *will* or *won't*.

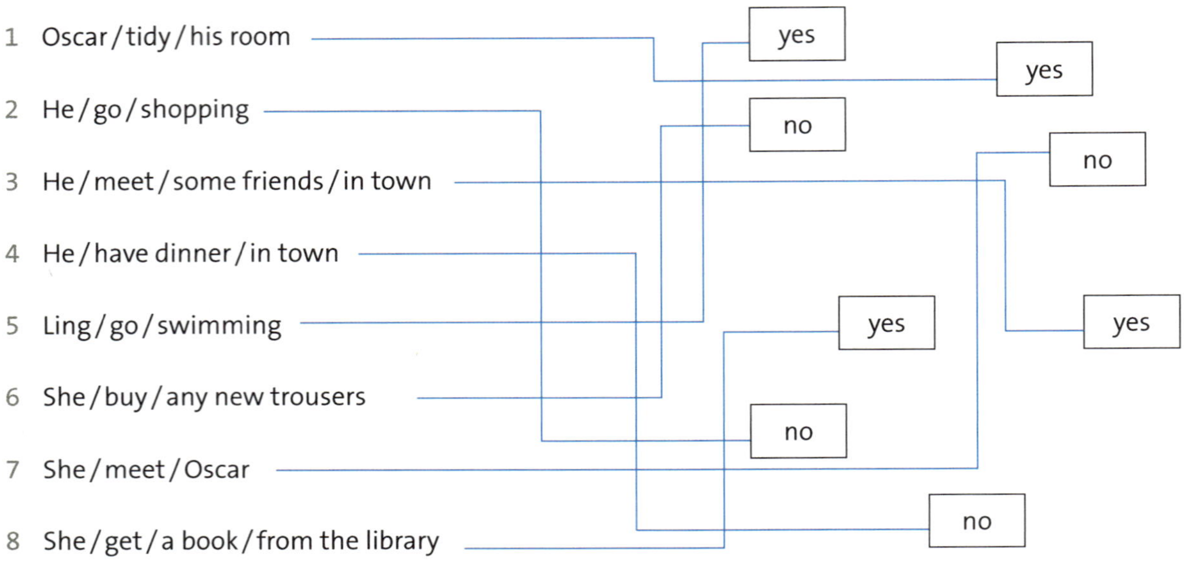

1 *Oscar will tidy his room.*
2 *He won't*
3
4
5 *Ling*
6 *She*
7
8

[1] **forecast** *Vorhersage*

7 Language Will-future Getting ready for a day in the country

► SB, p. 132

Complete the sentences with *'ll* or *won't*.

I want to go walking in the hills today. It's hot, so I ________ (1) need something to drink, but I ________ (2) need warm clothes. My friends Andy and Natalie are going to come with me, so I ________ (3) be alone. I ________ (4) need some money for the bus ticket home, of course. But I ________ (5) need a map because Natalie has a map app. There's a nice river on our way, so I ________ (6) take my swimming things. And I'm always hungry when I go walking, so I ________ (7) take some sandwiches, some fruit and some chocolate. I want to be sure that I ________ (8) be hungry this time!

8 Language Will-future A weekend in London

► SB, p. 132

Ling is talking to her cousin Flora.
Write *will*, *'ll* or *won't* + the right verb.

be • do • go • have • play • see • spend • ~~travel~~

Ling Tell me about your trip to London, Flora.

Flora Well, we'll travel to London by train on Saturday morning.

Ling Is it as long journey?

Flora Two hours. But it ____________ boring on the train, because I listen to a podcast when I travel. Or maybe I ____________ a game.

Ling And what W____________ you ____________ in London?

Flora During the day we ____________ the sights, and in the evening we ____________ to a show.

Ling And where W____________ you ____________ the night?

Flora At Uncle Ben's flat. But we ____________ a lot of time in London, because our train home leaves early on Sunday.

9 Chores in my family

► SB, p. 134

the rubbish • the dishwasher • the floors • my bed • my little brother • the table • the washing • my room • our pet cat • the clothes

a) Complete the sentences with word from the box.

1 I make ____________. E
2 I set ____________. ___
3 I babysit ____________. ___
4 I empty ____________. ___
5 I look after ____________. ___
6 I take out ____________. ___
7 I tidy ____________. ___
8 I vacuum ____________. ___
9 I fold ____________. ___
10 I do ____________. ___

b) Now write the right letter from pictures A–J next to each sentence in a).

10 The chores in Oscar's family

► SB, p. 135

Add the right endings to the verbs – if you have to!

> Remember in the simple present:
> He/She/It + verb + **s**
> We see. → He see**s**.
> They fly. → She fl**ies**. (consonant + y → -ies)
> You go. → He go**es**. (consonant + o → es)

1 Oscar *tidies* ______ (tidy) his room when it's messy and he sometimes ______ (babysit) at his neighbour's house.

2 His dad usually ______ (take) out the rubbish, and his mum or dad clean the bathroom.

3 Sometimes his dad ______ (do) the washing and sometimes his mum ______ (do) it.

4 Freddie ______ (empty) the dishwasher.

5 Olivia ______ (set) the table and Oscar's mum ______ (vacuum) the floors.

6 They all ______ (make) their own beds, but Oscar ______ (look) after the cat.

11 When are you free?

► SB, p. 135

Partner B: Look at page 88.

a) **Partner A: You want to meet Partner B after school.
Ask if he/she is free after school. If yes, write 'free'. If no, write why.**

Are you free after school on Monday/Tuesday/...?

Monday	Tuesday	Wednesday	Thursday	Friday
______	______	______	______	______

b) **Now look at your plans for the week. Then listen to your partner and answer him/her.**

Yes, I'm free.

No, sorry, I always ... on Monday/Tuesday/ ...

Monday	Tuesday	Wednesday	Thursday	Friday
 cook dinner	*free*	 lesson	 vacuum floors	*free*

c) **Now compare your information. On which day can you meet after school?** ______

12 Money words

▶ SB, p. 136

Match the yellow words and phrases with the blue ones. Write the complete sentences below.

get	*get money from*	*a cash machine*	*account*
have a savings	*save money*	*in a piggy bank*	*money apps*
spend money	*use*	*on sweets*	*pocket money*

1 I ______________________________.

2 I ______________________________.

3 I ______________________________.

4 I ______________________________.

5 I ______________________________.

6 I ______________________________.

13 Money

▶ SB, p. 136

Complete the sentences with words from the box.

coins • earn • gifts • machine • money • need • pocket • put • save • spend

How money comes in:

1 You get ____________ money from your parents in cash.

2 Your parents use a pocket money app and ____________ money on a card every month.

3 You ____________ money when you do chores for people.

4 You often get ____________ on special days, like Christmas, Eid al-Fitr or your birthday.

5 You have a card and get money from a cash ____________.

How money goes out:

6 You buy things you ____________ (like clothes) and things you like (like chocolate and games).

7 You ____________ money on treats like going to the cinema or going bowling.

8 You buy ____________ for your friends and family.

9 You ____________ your money for later in a savings account.

10 If you don't need them now, you put ____________ in a piggy bank at home.

14 LANGUAGE Word order Then and now

▶ SB, p. 137

a) **Read the tip box. Then write the sentences with the words in the right order.**

!

Word order in English is	subject	verb	object
	I	want to be	a programmer.

1 *a plumber / I / want to be*

___	___	___

2 I want to be a plumber because *earn / a lot of money / they*

I want to be a plumber because	___	___	___

3 And I think that *they / useful work / do*

And I think that	___	___	___

4 People are always happy when *arrives / a plumber*

People are always happy when	___	___

b) **Now read the German sentences and complete the English translations.**

1 *Ich will Menschen helfen. Vielleicht kann ich Krankenpfleger werden.*

want / I / people / to help *can / I / a nurse / be*

___	___	___	Maybe	___	___	___

2 *Ich will Zugfahrer sein, weil ich Züge mag.*

want to be / I / a train driver *trains / like / I*

___	___	___	because	___	___	___

3 *Als ich klein war, wollte ich Mechaniker werden. Jetzt will ich Architekt werden.*

I / little / was *wanted / I / a mechanic / to be*

When	___	___	___	___	___	___

want / I / an architect / to be

Now	___	___	___

15 Mediation Shopping

► SB p. 138

Mediate for Olivia, an English friend who is in a clothes shop in Germany. Write your sentences in German below.

Olivia	I have three questions. What size is this T-shirt?
You	______________________
Olivia	And do you have those jeans in black?
You	______________________
Olivia	Can I try on these trousers?
You	______________________
Shop assistant	Ja, sicher, alles kein Problem!

16 Shopping for clothes

► SB p. 138

a) **Read dialogue 1 with a partner.**

Josie	What size is this T-shirt?
Shop assistant	It's size M.
Josie	Do you have this T-shirt in blue?
Shop assistant	No, we don't. But that T-shirt is blue. Is it OK?
Josie	Great. Can I try it on?
Shop assistant	Yes, of course. *(Josie tries the T-shirt on.)*
Josie	OK, I'll take it. How much does this T-shirt cost?
Shop assistant	£12.99.

b) **Now complete dialogue 2. Use *these* and *those*.**

Josie	What size are __________ trousers?
Shop assistant	They are size M.
Josie	Do you have __________ trousers in blue?
Shop assistant	No, we don't. But __________ trousers are blue. Are they OK?
Josie	Great. Can I try them on?
Shop assistant	Yes, of course. *(Josie tries the trousers on.)*
Josie	OK, __________ trousers are perfect. I'll take them. How much do they cost?
Shop assistant	£38.99.

25 c) **Listen and check. Then read dialogue 2 with a partner.**

I can talk about money and shopping.

17 Tell the story of the video

► SB, p. 143

a) Match the people and the actions A–E. A person can have one or more actions.

A almost breaks something | B washed the clothes | C is at home
D folds the clothes best | E talks like an radio reporter[1]

Emir ________ Daisy ________ Joe ________ Emir's dad ________

b) Now check your answers with a partner.

I think Emir … | *Yes, I agree.* | *Really? I don't think so. I think Emir …*

c) VIEWING Now watch the video and check your answers.

18 VIEWING What's the missing word?

► SB, p. 143

Watch the video and write the missing words.

Part 1 (00:31 to 01:02)

1 Emir: 'Dad says I can't go out until I finish doing my *ch*____________.'

Part 2 (01:03 to 01:47)

2 Emir: 'I need to fold them before I can go *o*____________.'

3 Joe: 'Who wants to *t*____________?'

Part 3 (01:48 to 03:30)

4 Emir: 'He's fast. But can he be *t*____________?'

Part 4 (03:31 to 03:54)

5 Gloria: 'Oops! Don't break *a*____________!'

6 Emir: 'Do you think they will also do my *h*____________?'

19 Opinions

► SB, p. 143

Complete sentences 1 and 2. Then write your own opinion in sentence 3.

1 Joe and Daisy are really kind because ________________________________

2 Joe and Daisy are a bit stupid[2] because ________________________________

3 What do you think? ________________________________

[1] **radio reporter** *Rundfunkreporter/in* [2] **stupid** *dumm*

20 New verbs in Unit 5

Write the missing vowels.
Cross them in the box when you use them.

a • e • e • e • e • e • e • e •
i • i • o • o

1 Plumbers f _ x things in the bathroom, like toilets and showers.

2 You _ w n the things that you have bought.

3 Many people b _ l _ _ v _ in God.

4 Bakeries are shops that s _ l l bread.

5 People often miss their old house when they m _ v _ to a new one.

6 I'm sorry. I didn't understand what you said. Can you r _ p _ _ t it, please?"

21 Categories

a) **Write the words in the right lists.**

~~bakery~~ • bank • church • confident • excited • firefighter • hairdresser • hard-working • mosque • newsagent • nurse • plumber • rich • shop assistant • successful

places	jobs	describing people
bakery		

b) **Now write the correct words from part a).**

1 A shop where you can buy bread: ____________________

2 Somebody who cuts people's hair: ____________________

3 Doing well and having everybody's respect: ____________

4 A shop where you can buy sweets: ____________________

22 A short geography lesson

Write the two names.

1 **This is the ________________.**

2 **This is ________________.**

23 Wrong word!

Which word is wrong? Why?
Use words from the box to say why.

chore • clothes • job • money • ~~shop~~ • treat

1 bakery ~~office~~ charity shop newsagent ____________ is wrong, because it isn't a shop ____________.

2 plumber nurse customer hairdresser ____________ because it isn't a ____________.

3 clean tidy vacuum enjoy ____________ because it isn't a ____________.

4 size change cash coin ____________ because it isn't ____________.

5 stars shorts trousers suits ____________ because they aren't ____________.

6 gift chore screen time film ____________ because it isn't a ____________.

24 Letters that you don't say

a) In the words below, **highlight** the letters that you don't say.

business	plumber	comfortable	mechanic	sign	taught

26 b) Listen and check your answers.

c) Now say the words to your partner. Then swap roles.

25 Speak English well: TH

27 a) Voiced TH

Listen and repeat the words.
Tip: You can't whisper a voiced TH!

they, there, these, mother, another

I clean the windows and vacuum the floor.

28 b) Unvoiced TH

Listen and repeat the words.

teeth, thirty, thing, birthday

Think of your health!

29 c) Listen and repeat: voiced and unvoiced

1 Don't think too long about these things!

2 Both my brothers like buying clothes.

Voiced TH [ð] usually:
Start of function words: this, the, those, then
Middle of words: father, other
A difficult one: clothes

Unvoiced TH [θ] usually:
End of words: strength, north, month, health
Start of non-function words: think, theatre, three

Shhh! I'll tell you a secret: not everyone in Britain can say a TH! Some say 'vis', not 'this', or 'maffs' not 'maths'. So try to say TH – but it isn't tragic if you can't ☺.

The story in Unit 5:

My favourite character(s) in the story:

__________ because __________

I liked / didn't like the story in Unit 5 because __________

Some long words in Unit 5:

dishwasher

____

____

____

Jobs:

____

____

____

____

Money words: __________

I remember different chores: I __________

____

____

I can write a sentence with

- *will*: *(It will rain tomorrow.)*
- *won't*: __________
- *this/that*: __________
- *these/those*: __________
- word order with *because*: __________

What I can do better in English next year:

☐ reading ☐ writing ☐ listening ☐ speaking

1 The big predictions quiz

a) Tick (✓) one or more predictions about your future.

1 When I'm older:

A I'll stay in my town. ☐

B I'll stay in Germany. ☐

C I'll live in a different country. ☐

D I'll live in many different countries. ☐

2 When I'm older:

A People won't use coins any more. ☐

B People won't use cars any more. ☐

C People will have no work. ☐

D Robots will vacuum our houses. ☐

3 When I'm older:

A I'll have three children or more. ☐

B I won't get married. ☐

C I'll get married and have children. ☐

D I won't have any children. ☐

4 When I'm older:

A I'll earn a lot of money. ☐

B I'll save and buy my own house. ☐

C I'll travel around the world. ☐

D Money won't be too important for me. ☐

5 When I'm older:

A I'll be a hairdresser. ☐

B I'll be an artist. ☐

C I'll be a footballer. ☐

D I'll be famous. ☐

E Not A, B, C or D ☐

6 When I'm older:

A I want to have my own business. ☐

B I'll be a computer programmer. ☐

C I'll work in the film business. ☐

D I want a job where I can be creative. ☐

E Not A, B, C or D ☐

b) Now compare with other students in class. Who has the most predictions the same as you?

Unit 1 Topic 2 | Exercise 9

► WB, p. 12 ► SB, p. 18

a) Partner B: Look at the information and read the train station announcements[1].

The next train to Brighton is at 14.13 at platform 2.
Platform 2 for the 14.13 train to Brighton.

The next train to ... is at ... at platform ...
Platform ... for the ... train to ...

The next train ...

Brighton 14.13	Platform 2
Hastings 14.21	Platform 5
Eastbourne 14.03	Platform 5
Portsmouth 14.09	Platform 4

b) The train to Brighton is late. Look at the information and answer your partner's question.

I'm sorry, the 14.13 train to Brighton is late.
The new arrival time is ...
And it doesn't arrive at platform ...,
but at platform ...

Brighton 14.13	Platform 2
New arrival time:	14.45
Platform change:	Platform 1

c) Now listen to your partner. Write the times of the trains.

Train to Woking: ___________

Train to Gatwick Airport: ___________

Train to Epsom: ___________

Train to Dorking: ___________

d) Now ask your partner about the train to Dorking. Write the answer.

Excuse me, please.
Do I need to change trains for Dorking?

Answer: ____

e) Now check your answers with your partner.

[1] **announcement** *Ansage*

Unit 2 Topic 3 | Exercise 13

► WB, p. 31 ► SB, p. 50

a) Your partner has a picture of a weird superhero. Ask your partner questions about it. Then draw it in the box on the right.

How many	heads	eyes	does it have?
	noses	feet	
	hands	teeth	

How many heads does it have?

It has two heads.

b) Now look at your picture of a superhero. Answer your partner's questions about it.

c) Now look at your partner's picture. Is your picture the same?

Unit 4 Topic 1 | Exercise 4

► WB, p. 57 ► SB, p. 101

a) Partner B: Look at what you have for a picnic. Then listen to your partner and answer him/her.

No problem, I have some …

Sorry, I don't have any …

✓

✗

✓

✓

✗

✓

b) Now tell your partner more things that you need for a picnic. Listen to your partner. Put a tick (✓) if your partner has it. Put an ✗ if not.

We also need some …

carrots?	☐	apples?	☐
ham?	☐	cheese?	☐
biscuits	☐	cake?	☐

c) Now write what you and your partner still need.

We still need *some* *some*

Unit 5 Topic 2 | Exercise 10

► WB. p. 77 ► SB, p. 135

a) Partner B: Partner A wants to meet you after school. Look at your plans for the week. Listen to your partner and answer him/her.

Yes, I'm free.

No, sorry, I always ... on Monday/Tuesday/ ...

Monday	Tuesday	Wednesday	Thursday	Friday
free	 look after the dog	 club	 clean the bathroom	*free*

b) Now ask your partner if he/she is free after school. If yes, write 'free'. If no, write why.

Are you free after school on Monday/Tuesday/...?

Monday	Tuesday	Wednesday	Thursday	Friday

c) Now compare your information. On which day can you meet after school? ____________